GOD BELONGS IN BUSINESS

Twelve Kingdom Principles for Life and Business

FOREWORD BY DANIELLA ORDONEZ

All rights reserved. No part of this publication may be reproduced, distributed, or transmitted in any form or by any means, including photocopying, recording, or other electronic or mechanical methods, without the prior written permission of the publisher, except in the case of brief quotations embodied in critical reviews and certain other noncommercial uses permitted by copyright law. For permission requests, please contact the publisher.

Scripture quotations marked (NKJV) are taken from the New King James Version®. Copyright © 1982 by Thomas Nelson. Used by permission. All rights reserved.

THE HOLY BIBLE, NEW INTERNATIONAL VERSION®, NIV® Copyright © 1973, 1978, 1984, 2011 by Biblica, Inc.® Used by permission. All rights reserved worldwide.

Scripture quotations marked (NLT) are taken from the Holy Bible, New Living Translation, copyright © 1996, 2004, 2007. Used by permission of Tyndale House Publishers Inc., Carol Stream, Illinois 60188. All rights reserved.

Scripture quotations marked (KJV) are taken from the Holy Bible, King James Version, Public Domain.

Scripture quotations marked (KJ21) are taken from the 21st Century King James Version®, copyright © 1994. Used by permission of Deuel Enterprises, Inc., Gary, SD 57237. All rights reserved.

Scripture quotations marked (NRSV) are taken from the New Revised Standard Version Updated Edition. Copyright © 2021 National Council of Churches of Christ in the United States of America. Used by permission. All rights reserved worldwide.

The views and opinions expressed are those of individual authors and do not necessarily reflect the official policy or position of Tell Your Story nor other authors and companies included in the publication.

This collaboration was curated and produced by Tell Your Story Coaching

Acknowledgments

All glory goes to the Father who uniquely created each of the authors presented in this book.

This book would not have been possible without the team that helped put it together. Thank you to every one of you who are a part of Tell Your Story Coaching and Network for the Kingdom. Your efforts do not go unnoticed.

FOREWORD
DANIELLA ORDONEZ 1

INFLUENCE THROUGH DOMINION
PATRICIO ORDONEZ, USA 5

FREEDOM AND LEGACY
CRISTINA GUTIERREZ, USA 19

OBEDIENCE PRODUCES BLESSINGS
EVANGELINE PESCASIO, USA 33

STEWARDSHIP - A MESSAGE FOR YOU
LORRAINE WOODS, USA.. 49

STEWARDSHIP
LENORA STONE, USA 63

GOD'S TRUTH THROUGH SIMPLICITY
VALERY B. IRELAND, USA 83

TRUTH AND REST
JANET TAYLOR, USA 99

INTEGRITY - WHO'S GOING TO KNOW?
ELIZABETH KIRSTEN, UK 115

GRATITUDE UNLEASHED
SONJA CHRISTINE, USA 131

A SPIRIT OF GRATITUDE
NESTOR GOMEZ, USA 153

AUTHENTICITY - DESTRUCTION TO RADICAL DESTINY
CHRIS PORTER, UK.. 173

FAITH IS KEY
MARY WESTCOTT, USA 189

WORKS CITED 207

Foreword

It is with great pleasure that we bring forward *God Belongs in Business*. This is the first collaborative book of many to come written, produced, and marketed on behalf of *Network for the Kingdom*, its partners, affiliates, mentors, and friends. We truly believe this book will revolutionize several key areas of influence. I've had the honor of being able to work with each of the authors in different capacities, whether in business, coaching, partnerships, mentorships, or ministerial capacities. Each of the authors truly has a heart after God to honor Him in all that they do. Each one is an expert in their area of influence in their own right. This book is a reflection of the diverse backgrounds, talents, gifts, and individual callings placed on each author like the diverse nature of the Body of Christ. *Network for the Kingdom* has always sought to provide a platform to highlight individuals in their unique offerings for which they were created to serve others.

The ministry marketplace is a term that some have become keen on in recent years, although this is not something new. God is everywhere. At the time of writing this foreword, I had recently seen a play that expanded my thinking in many ways. It showed the life of the prophet Daniel. In one scene, we see the pre-incarnate Christ standing in the fire with Shadrach, Meshach, and Abednego when they were commanded to be thrown into the furnace. Earlier played a scene of the prophet Ezekiel, proclaiming that we should not place God in a box and that He could be there with

Daniel in his trials, and He is not merely contained to the mercy seat in the temple. God could be anywhere He pleased and so it was true. God was just as present in Jerusalem as He was in the fire with the young men who refused to bow to the golden idol. This is also true for the areas of our lives in which we invite God to come and partake. God can be with the pastor in the pulpit as much as He can be with and minister through the entrepreneur who set out to change the world for the Kingdom. This means, despite the opinions of some, God undoubtedly is involved in our business ventures. In fact, we see this is the case when Peter is commanded to cast his net on the other side of his boat and so bring in a harvest of fish, when before he could catch none. At the outset, it is clear that the physical fish, cleaned and sold, would generate a profit, while simultaneously a prophetic act concerning fishing for the souls of mankind. It is foolish to assume that God does not care about our businesses and the ways in which we conduct them. This also means allowing for the marketplace to serve as a place of ministry. This is a hard pill to swallow for some and I highly recommend reading *Creating Wealth for the Kingdom: Heal your relationship with money and fund the mission of Christ.* That book deals with some of the misconceptions around faith and money from a biblical perspective. For many years there has been a mentality that God and business do not belong together, but this is not biblical as there are countless scriptures that deal with how we should do business by incorporating Kingdom principles and we will see our endeavors prosper.

Each of the authors have a unique perspective based on their experience, area of influence, and a Kingdom principle they have applied to their lives and businesses that helped them to see forward movement. Kingdom principles are not just for us but serve as a witness to the Risen King who has given us all that we need for life and godliness.

"According to His divine power hath given unto us all things that pertain unto life and godliness, through the knowledge of Him that hath called us to glory and virtue." - 2 Peter 1:3, KJV

When we partner with God in our business, we can trust that not only will there be an impact here on Earth, but one in the Heavens. We've all had experiences with those who did not abide by Kingdom principles. I can give you countless examples of dealing with dishonest salespeople, co-workers with negative attitudes, and the Human Resources representative who made me feel like I was of little value to the company. This is not God's design for business.

It is only through God's principles and those who abide by them, that the world can experience sustainable change. God truly does belong in business. I hope that whether you are starting a new business venture, have an interest in entrepreneurship, or are an established business expert, you will take something out of this book you can apply to those who are connected to you and will apply these principles in your everyday life. Numbers 23:19 assures us, "God is not a man that He should lie; neither the son of man, that he should repent: hath He said, and shall He not do it? Or hath He spoken, and shall He not make it good" (KJV). When we apply these principles, we can rest assured that we will see progress and forward advancement in our lives and businesses. Start applying these Kingdom principles today to be the change you want to see in the world and a change that is everlasting as we do our part in bringing the Kingdom everywhere we are called, unashamedly and without hesitation.

Daniella Ordonez
Curator of God Belongs in Business
Co-Founder Network for the Kingdom

CHAPTER 1

Influence Through Dominion

Patricio Ordonez, USA

VISIONARY LEADERSHIP COACH

My business started as an idea from God. My wife, Daniella Ordonez, and I had an idea to create a group that would impact people. We didn't think about creating an income out of it in the beginning. Over time, we realized that it was possible. One day, my wife was cleaning, and she received an idea to start Network for the Kingdom. This group would serve as a stage/platform for others. This is where we help people scale their business through stages. When we first started out, we were struggling to get clients. It was hard to get on platforms if you didn't have a ton of followers. We decided to help other Kingdom entrepreneurs get visibility and possibly gain clients at the same time. We have always dreamed of being on stage to impact others with our message but didn't understand the process of how to do it. We knew others had to be struggling with this problem as well. In the beginning, we held so many challenges (a marketing strategy). We found our tribe after much trial and error. Shortly after, we launched *Tell Your Story Coaching*, where we teach people how to write a book and launch a business with the book. This was another God idea. It took a lot of effort, but we eventually hit the ground running. We've seen countless clients step into dominion through their unique message.

Dominion is directly connected with influence. We have seen clients come in and land high-ticket clients. They've closed contracts that secured their salary for the whole year. That is what happens when you step into the area of influence where you've been called to take dominion. You have the solution to a real problem. Many of you have been called to have a global impact and that means you need a clear vision and mission for your business. Global dominion means you will need to have self-control and authority over all aspects of your life. This can only happen when you understand and apply the principles of Kingdom dominion. Myron Golden has been heard teaching that you can create a massive amount of wealth in a short period of time. The nine-to-five mindset teaches you how to create wealth over long stretches of time. I believe Kingdom entrepreneurs can create massive amounts of wealth in a short period of time. We are free to create and build with God. This means building up His people and spreading the dominion of the church. Dr. Myles Monroe was a teacher beyond his time, and he spoke often about these things.

Dr. Myles Monroe uses a great example of how God's laws can truly benefit our lives. He spoke about the aerodynamics of an airplane. He explained how the plane takes off, including the needed speed. He explained that when the airplane takes off at around 160 mph, then it needs to maintain that speed because, at a certain height, the law of gravity is eliminated. The law of gravity at this point works to propel you higher. If you were to just stop, then the plane would be crushed into pieces. God has created laws for us to benefit from and when we understand and apply them, we are propelled to go higher.

Charles Capps speaks about the Dominion Principle. He tells us that the Word, which is the incorruptible seed, displays the dominion factor. The seed has dominion over the soil. The soil has no choice but to respond to the seed (God's Word) and to produce in your life. Capps explains, "What gives one such power to have that kind of victory, and to exercise dominion over the world? Such victory comes through faith. Faith is the principle of dominion, that principle that gives you the victory to overcome, and keeping things under your control" (Capps). God has set the bar high for our lives and given us everything we need to be successful. Jesus came and died for our sins. Reaching God apart from Christ is impossible. The standard has been set. Jesus came and took back the dominion that was lost by Adam and Eve in the Garden of Eden. He did this for us, and freely gave it to us. God restored what was lost.

God wants His children to be leaders. We need to walk in the truth knowing and understanding that our time here is temporary. We must make an impact in the Earth; an impact so big that His name will be praised through our obedient actions. God is the King and has given dominion to His children. This means stepping into our roles of leaders who lead with excellence, working through our highest potential, and not leaving anything behind or only halfway done. Dominion involves conquering territory, but in the Kingdom, it means bringing the ways of the Kingdom wherever we go. Your gifts are for others, and you have been called to bring His light into the darkness. For many of you, that means bringing the Kingdom into the marketplace. You have been called to take dominion in that area.

When you understand your God-given dominion, you will know freedom and power. People crave power because in many cases it makes a person feel free. It also helps them to make decisions that will impact future generations. You have the freedom to make decisions and to bring others into alignment with Kingdom principles. Kingdom dominion unleashes the power of God and transforms wherever you are and whatever you encounter. Dominion transcends understanding and multiplies your authority. Dominion gives you the ability to create wealth and manage a team. It gives you the ability to restore, retain, and regain any aspect of the marketplace. Dr. Myles Monroe defines dominion as the ability to govern, rule, control, manage, lead, and master.

In other words:

"And God said, Let us make man in our image, after our likeness: and let them have dominion over the fish of the sea, and over the fowl of the air, and over the cattle, and over all the earth, and over every creeping thing that creepeth upon the earth."- Genesis 1:26, KJV

Every person wants to feel powerful. Powerlessness has led to a lot of problems in our world. People search for it in religion, and within themselves. Yet God has given us the ability to govern through the principle of dominion. People

Influence Through Dominion

yearn to feel powerful because they were created for dominion. Apart from God, they will never know true power. When you don't know the dominion you are given through Jesus then you don't use your light to shape the culture. Instead, you will bring your pain and cause destruction. We are called for more than that.

Dominion does not mean dictatorship. It means elevating others so that they can see Jesus. When we are wrapped in the love of Jesus, we can step into power, prosperity, and protection. Through His love, we can go to higher ground. Dominion tells us to go higher. We are called to higher levels of understanding. We are called to impact, move, shape, reconstruct, tear down, plant, and grow for the Kingdom. Dominion helps you to define the culture, movement, income, marketing, and retention of your customers and team.

THE PRINCIPLE OF DOMINION BROKEN UP INTO SEVEN PARTS:

1. Government
2. Rule
3. Control
4. Management
5. Mastery
6. Leadership
7. Power

THE SEVEN PARTS APPLIED TO THREE CORE AREAS OF DOMINION:

1. Self   2. Marketplace   3. Global

SELF-DOMINION

We have a need only God can meet, but God has given us principles through which we can dominate the area we have been called to impact. Self-dominion involves disciplining yourself to the point of self-constraint or self-control. I like to do cold plunges. These are baths that are -60°. When I plunge into the water, my brain tells me *"What are you doing? You need to get out of this place right now".* Your brain is trying to protect you from experiencing pain. Self-dominion goes against the nature of pain. The pain process forms your character necessary to go through. God never leaves anything behind because He turns pain into purpose. Pain can be a motivator to push you to the next level. Self-dominion means having self-control over your mental, emotional, physical, and spiritual life. It requires discipline. Discipline is the bridge that unites you with your dreams and your goals. Discipline makes it easy and enjoyable to reach those dreams and visions. Discipline is costly because it requires you to step out of your comfort zone daily, but once you build it, then you're able to maintain the changes in your life. I wake up at 5 a.m. every morning because I want to experience the freedom of reaching my dreams. This looks like having a schedule every single day. You should be growing every day in whatever area God has called you. Become a student of life. This is an important step in becoming powerful. We are able to be more in control of the situations around us. When you set your foundation for the day, you can build a path to maintain the peace of God within us. Discipline is hard to start, but easy to maintain once you've done it.

"But I discipline my body and bring it into subjection, lest, when I have preached to others, I myself should become disqualified." - 1 Corinthians 9:27, NKJV

Self-dominion starts with getting on your knees and asking Him to give you the desire to do it. When you learn to master one area, you're able to move on to the next area of dominion which involves the marketplace. If you can master your world, you can master the marketplace.

Marketplace Dominion

Marketplace dominion refers to a state of market leadership, dominance, or control, where a business, organization, or individual has a significant influence or supremacy in a particular market or industry. It implies a position of strength and authority to shape the market, set trends, and influence consumer behavior. Your business is a model of who you are emotionally, physically, and spiritually. The way you carry yourself will be reflected in your business.

The marketplace is a place where only a few survive for the long term.

You do not have to be famous to dominate the market. You can do really well in your area of expertise by becoming the best version of yourself. For some, this means having a goal of $1,000,000 and for others it's $100,000 and for others it's $10,000. No matter who or where you are, you're going to crush it! Dominating the marketplace does not require you to have a certificate of accomplishment. It takes drive, determination, commitment, and consistency. When we place these ingredients together, we will dominate. Dominion in the marketplace means showing up for the ones you serve when others haven't shown up for them.

There is a powerful rule known as the 99/1. When referring to the 99/1 rule, we are talking about one person out there who is fascinated by your message. Someone who is receiving everything you share because you are speaking their unique language. Jesus said in John 10:27, "My sheep hear my voice, and I know them, and they follow me" (NKJV). When you know your audience, you can call them out by their name and that is the most powerful way to gain mastery in your market. This also means becoming known for one thing. *What have you been dreaming about? What keeps you up*

Influence Through Dominion

at night? What motivates you? What topic are you constantly talking to your friends about? It takes five years to become a master of something. Master the art of your natural influence then nurture the growth daily. Create the habit of discipline and this will help you to reach your full potential. *How far will you be by the end of the year? Will you reach your goals or are you trying to master everything and, in the end, become a master of none?*

Marketplace dominion means giving your best presentation. Offer something distinctive and valuable that sets you apart. Create offers that separate you from any other person. Serve them very well to the point that they will continue to come back. Serve them the best meal they've ever had in their entire life, and it will return to you. I remember one time when my wife and I went to a restaurant for our anniversary. I remember we sat down together and the first thing the waiter did was greet us with a smile. The surroundings were breathtaking: lake view, sunset, and a mountain. The waiter brought us food, and the presentation and service were unforgettable. He knew if he was going to serve us well, we would always remember the moment and the presentation. He brought us complimentary glasses of champagne, offered to a take photo, and was there for everything we needed.

When you deliver your presentation, make sure you deliver a product or service at high quality. First impressions are very important and serving people well is following God's principles.

Global Dominion

Global dominion means worldwide reach. Amazon dominates the online space, and this is part of the global marketplace. You might wonder how you can reach that broad of an audience and how you can take dominion like Amazon. Understand the value of what you carry. There are billions of people in the world and there are people praying for your product/service to be released. There are people praying for your message to be heard. They are praying for you to reach them so you can help them to overcome their pain.

We dominate when we know and understand we have a Kingdom economy, and our King owns it all. God has the ability to prosper you faster than any man has ever seen just like He did with Solomon. God can give you a dream, and the ability to create wealth, but we must rely on the Kingdom's economy. When I talk about the Kingdom economy, I am referring to His principles, laws, and revelations. Kingdom economy refers to an economic model of a system based on biblical principles and values, prioritizing the well-being of other people. We are to rely on His Kingdom economy rather than the one of this world. Kingdom economics is about managing resources well and honoring God through them. When we help others benefit, God helps us to make it successful. In the Kingdom economy, there is stewardship, management of blessings, and multiplication.

Global dominion means creating a market shift. You must become a disruptor for the Kingdom. We must learn to become disruptors to the point that we create a market shift, but in order to become this, we must seek the ideas of the King. God has ideas for us in wisdom, so we can have dominion globally for the Kingdom of God creating a major shift in the market. This requires us to think outside of the box beyond what we can imagine. Most of the imagination comes from the King who has the solutions to fix our problems. We must learn how to shift and navigate the market to stay ahead and relevant in the face of e-commerce changes, AI, and other marketplace disruptors. Global marketplace dominion is important to leave a generational legacy for our children's children. We must break generational curses and go deeper to leave a legacy for the generations to come. Solving the world's problems with Kingdom keys unlocks truths necessary for progress. God has given us these keys and we must learn how to use them in partnership with the revelations given to us by the King.

ABOUT THE AUTHOR

Patricio is married to the most amazing woman in the world. He is the father of two future entrepreneurs and is a Kingdom entrepreneur himself. He is a second-time author with the release of *God Belongs in Business,* his first book, also a collaborative project titled, *Creating Wealth for the Kingdom*. He is passionate about creating highly profitable businesses and has an unwavering commitment to excellence. Patricio loves sharing his wealth of knowledge and experience with aspiring Kingdom entrepreneurs and influencers. Through his writing, he seeks to inspire and empower others to pursue their entrepreneurial dreams and achieve sustainable success in the competitive business landscape.

TO CONNECT WITH PATRICIO:

Email: connect@network4thekingdom.com
Instagram: @thestorybusinesscoach
YouTube: www.youtube.com/@patricio2459
Facebook: Network for the Kingdom
　　　　　Tell Your Story Coaching (Books to Business)

OTHER BOOKS: *CREATING WEALTH FOR THE KINGDOM*

CHAPTER 2

Freedom And Legacy

Cristina Gutierrez, USA
LEGACY FOUNDATION CRAFTING COACH

On a Saturday morning, my husband Mario and I decided to drive to the city to go grocery shopping. Our young twenty-year-old selves decided to drive to the city for a little more excitement because we lived in a small town with not many shopping options. The 45-mile drive was perfect for deep conversations between two young dreamers. That Saturday sure was unforgettable. As the day came to an end, we came across a Ford dealership. My dream car has always been a Ford Mustang, and the Ford dealership had Mustangs lined up ready to take on the streets. We decided to go check them out and admire their beauty. We always did. We would stop at any dealership to daydream of what would be ours one day. Three hours later, after sitting in a chair with emotions of excitement running down my body, we drove home a bright orange Mustang! Orange was not my color. The salesman, who viewed us as a big commission check, was kind enough to let us drive home this bright orange Mustang. Our brand-new white Mustang with black accessories, curves perfectly sculpted, giving it an aerodynamic and sporty look was to be shipped from another city to this car lot.

As young twenty-year-olds, we were crushing our dreams one by one. *Well, at least we thought we were.* We had the house, the cars, and what is expected to follow - DEBT. How come no one talked about this monster? Don't get me wrong, there is good debt and bad debt, but neither of these was ever talked about in school or my household.

My passion for building a financial foundation came when I realized we were not able to enjoy our lives to the fullest. Everyone seemed to have it all together. Why didn't we?

Why build a financial foundation? Because it creates freedom. Galatians 5:1 says we were called to be free! We are so focused on doing things the way everyone else does because of a fear of missing out. Everyone is in this "timeline" you have to follow, and we feel like we must jump on it before it's too late. But we still lacked money to go out and do all the fun stuff. That's when I realized that we were building without a financial foundation. In the process of establishing my own foundation for personal development, I want to help you through your own journey.

As my relationship with God grew, I realized that He is the main foundation to anything. Mario and I were at a stage of building our own values and beliefs as a family. After attending many other churches trying to find a home, my co-worker then, best friend now, kept inviting us over to her church. On a random Saturday night in 2018, we decided we would go visit this church and surprise my friend. We did not know what to expect, but that day things inside of us happened. There was an awakening in our hearts. Thanks to my friend we found the best foundation, our relationship with God.

But remember the Lord your God, for it is He who gives you the ability to produce wealth, and so confirms His covenant, which He swore to your ancestors, as it is today.

- Deuteronomy 8:18, NKJV

God has given us the ability to produce wealth. Learning who I am in Christ has allowed me to recognize finances are part of my purpose.

My career in finance started a decade ago. I became a customer service representative and teller at my first banking job. I loved it. It was fun!

Two years later I moved towns and started working at a different bank. Here is where my story unfolds. I did not have clarity about my purpose. I did know that budgeting, banking, filing, and creating plans brought me so much joy. But I wanted more. There was more and I was hungry for it.

When you are in the Kingdom you connect with amazing people. I met Adolfo Martens through a Facebook post that was shared by one of my mentors. After digging through his Facebook page and seeing what he was all about I decided that he could help us. Adolfo set up a plan to become debt-free through life insurance. After that Mario and I started applying Kingdom principles to our own finances. Little did we know that there was still more!

Later in life, God introduced me to insurance as a career! I started getting clarity on what God's purpose was for me. I left the bank to go work for a well-known insurance company. Due to company regulations, I realized it would not allow me to expand using life insurance to become debt-free. This career shift has been one of the toughest I have encountered. I would question God, *Am I still doing the right thing? Did I hear you correctly? Is this really what you need me to do? If He brought me here, why am I not being successful?* There were things I needed to learn from that place so I could move on to my own business as an insurance agent. I left the company and partnered with other Kingdom entrepreneurs. Not only did this bring me acceleration, but it brought clarity, and more open doors to helping me create my coaching program that will guide you into becoming debt-free, building a financial foundation, and creating generational wealth. I am passionate about telling my story to young couples who are just getting started in the adult world because Mario and I were in that same spot when we first got married in our early twenties.

Everyone has unique gifts given by God, and one of my prominent attributes is the ability to instill trust. Establishing trust in matters of wealth and finances holds significant importance. My dedication to valuing and honoring every relationship reinforces a commitment to earning and maintaining your trust throughout our interactions. In the realm of my business, these fundamental principles play a crucial role. I not only earn people's trust to oversee your finances but also reveal the true essence of God within me. Because you are made in His image, every time you encounter a Kingdom entrepreneur not only do you meet the person, but also meet with a different piece of God.

If money was not a factor, what would you be doing right now? This question can have endless answers. It did for me: travel, go to college, help people, and the list goes on. But despite my answers all I saw and felt was FREEDOM. It brings me back to a dream I had when I was little. It was like a movie scene. I had won the golden ticket to Walmart. I had ten minutes to do whatever I wanted inside the store. I was in the food aisle. It was big, long, and illuminated by all the food coolers. I was determined to taste everything I could reach in ten minutes with no one telling me "no." Before the ten minutes started, I was envisioning myself full of the yummy food I had devoured to the point I could no longer walk. I don't remember if my ten minutes ever started, but I do remember feeling the freedom I had from no one ever telling me "No."

DEBT WILL TELL YOU "NO."

I learned that money was just a tool. I like to envision money as a hammer. With a hammer, you can either build things or destroy them. Same thing with money. You can grab the handle of your "money hammer" and gain control of what is going to happen next.

My financial freedom started with healing. God healed my heart when it came to money. Noelle Schwantes wrote a book called *Change Your $tory*. Noelle took me on a healing journey about finances. *"What do you mean I have to heal around money?"*

Going back to my dream as a little girl in the middle of the Walmart aisle I always thought that there was no way I could ever have the ability to taste anything and everything I wanted. Then, later in life, I realized I could. I bought everything that would satisfy me, but that led me nowhere financially. I was not using my money wisely. My financial tree was growing without being fruitful. I didn't understand why I was good with finances, but I never saw any fruit until I touched the root of my tree, healing from the inside out.

"Financial abundance is not about how much you have; it is about the peace you have." – Noelle Schwantes

Peace in my heart about money allowed me to listen to God on how to distribute it. It is about understanding the purpose of money. Tithing and offering became my priority. Giving did not only allow me to learn to give, but to also to let go. Like Patricio Ordonez said, *"Tithing is like having a joint bank account with God."* That was no joke. God provides for you above and beyond if you lean into Him. My husband and I can attest to that. Because we were stewarding His money well, He gave us more than we could imagine. Giving became like a magic trick to our finances. Our income was the same, but God would always multiply it. One way or another there was always enough for our needs, but also enough to bring blessings to others.

Honor the Lord with your wealth, with the first fruits of all your crops; then your barns will be filled to overflowing, and your vats will brim over with new wine. - Proverbs 3:9-10, NIV

When God spoke to my husband and me to give, we would have a little fun with it. We would individually ask, *"What is it, and how much, God?"* Once we got a number through listening, we would type it in our phone's calculator then show each other at the same time to reveal the amount of money we were supposed to give to that person, place, or charity. Not only was it fun to see how God spoke to us in the same way, but it brought joy in connecting with one another and knowing that we were stewarding well as one in marriage. Giving brought joy to us. Most importantly, we had the freedom to do so!

"You want to find out what all your issues are? Start a business. It has a knack for bringing up known and unknown insecurities!" - Noelle Schwantes

We cannot allow our fears and insecurities to stop us from building. Start the business. Start the book. Take action.

5 Steps To Help You Take Action:

STEP 1: SURROUND YOURSELF WITH A COMMUNITY

It is important to surround yourself with people who have the same mindset or goals you have. They will encourage and help you through the resistance you will come across. It's encouraging to see other people pay down debt. This will spark energy for you to continue with your debt-free journey.

STEP 2: WRITE IT DOWN

Writing down any idea or goal will be the first action you need to help you keep track of your finances. Write down all your debt and arrange them from the lowest to highest amount owed and start focusing on paying off one debt at a time. This will allow you to monitor your progress.

STEP 3: SHARE WITHIN YOUR COMMUNITY

Once you start sharing with your community, you will find people who have similar stories and solutions to some of your problems. Allowing others to help you will make the journey easier.

Step 4: Be present for yourself

Become your own cheerleader. It is *you* vs. *you*. No one will limit you down the road, but yourself. Being present will help your confidence. You will feel unstoppable after seeing the results of your financial plan.

Step 5: Do it!

I always hear *just do it*! But it did not make sense to me. I would pray, "God, what does 'just do it' look like?" God answered, "Like faith." At that moment I realized I had to trust Him. I opened up Microsoft Word and started typing. God started unloading visions, ideas, and strategies as I typed. Like this book collaboration, I had no idea what I was going to write but I took action and "just did it." I envision listening to God like the action step a stenographer does, the person who is typing everything they are saying at the courthouse during a hearing. Your action step is to place the paper into the typewriter's rollers. (A typewriter is a machine with keys they used before computers). Next is to listen and start typing. You will be building a financial foundation for you and generations to come!

Remember there is always room to grow. No matter what financial situation you find yourself in, it is never too late to be set free in your finances. It is a journey to which you must commit. Any baby steps taken toward your financial goals will give you tremendous success.

I found myself at the store once and thought, "Well, it's just five dollars," and purchased the unnecessary thing I had in my hand. A day later I was scrambling through my purse looking for three dollars as I sat in the parking lot of our local tortilleria (A tortilleria is a shop that sells freshly made tortillas). It was lunchtime and nothing beats fresh tortillas. As I sat there with the three dollars in my hand God spoke to me and allowed me to see how a three dollar product kept a business going. I started viewing any amount of money I had differently and because something cost less than five dollars did not mean it was worth it.

You need to be aware of your spending or the debt you have before you can make any changes. Fall in love with this journey allowing the *financial freedom* feeling to set you free from the moment you decide to change. Give it to God!

God is ready to give you wealth. He is ready for you to tap into who He is in you. Discover the treasures within you. Every detail about you is a treasure that will level you up to reach His wealth. Why? Because the more you fulfill your purpose the more availability you have to His riches.

Freedom and Legacy

"Our God is able to do exceedingly abundantly above all that we ask or think"- Ephesians 3:20, NKJV

Everything you do, do it for yourself. Do it for the legacy you leave behind. Do it for the freedom you will unleash. You only have one life. Make the best of it! It is meant to be enjoyed.

Level up with the financial freedom to better fulfill your purpose. Allow money to be a tool in your life to get prosperous results. The time is now! Go on the journey because you are worthy.

About the Author

Cristina Gutierrez is a financial coach whose life experiences have driven her to help others overcome debt. She has been married to her amazing husband for seven years and has a son. With her experience in banking, she seeks God's voice for strategies and guidance in helping others build a strong financial foundation. Cristina is also helping others find solutions to their needs through health and life insurance.

To Connect with Cristina:

Email: cristinaginsurnace@gmail.com
Facebook: Cristina Gutierrez, Insurance Agent

CHAPTER 3

Obedience Produces Blessings

Evangeline Pescasio, USA
LIFE AND HEALTH TRANSFORMATION COACH, RN, NBC-HWC

"He that hath my commandments, and keepeth them, he it is that loveth me: and he that loveth me shall be loved of my Father, and I will love him, and will manifest myself to him."
- John 14:21, KJV

As tears flowed down my face, and heaviness consumed my heart, I found myself on my knees, desperately crying out to God. With my hands lifted, I muttered, *"I can no longer do it on my own. I surrender everything to you, Lord."*

I was in this posture when I felt Jesus' arms wrapped around me as He said, *"I love you."* That was all I needed, and in that place, my healing journey started. Up until that time, I didn't realize how growing up in poverty, yelling, shaming, lack of emotional connection, and rejection wounded my heart. I wasn't aware those wounds were getting in the way of God's plan for my life affecting every relationship I had.

Over the past thirty years of working in health care and helping people heal, I've had the privilege of having deep, meaningful conversations and asking people about their "why." For many, the most important thing is their family, their children, and their legacy.

I have been through difficult seasons in my life that led me to reflect on and change my "why." When I first fell in love and got married at a young age, my husband became the center of my universe. When my kids were born, they became my main reason to live. I now have grown children, and I am excited for my future grandchildren. When they arrive, I'm almost sure they will take most of my time.

I love my family, especially my children, who are God's most precious gifts to me, but as my faith grows, I realize we can't love anyone or anything more than we love God. I want to love God more than anything or anyone, and I want to be obedient to what He has called me to do. I know my family is my first ministry, but I do not want to use them as an excuse not to pursue the higher purpose God has for me.

Despite the difficult seasons I've been through, I am blessed that God's power, mercy, and grace enabled me to overcome childhood trauma, poverty, rejection, and depression. When I experienced God's love and healing from depression, I told God I didn't want to be away from Him ever again. I want to be obedient to Him, serve Him, and use the gifts He has given me to honor Him. This is why I'm passionate about helping people overcome their adversities, and experience breakthroughs. Serving is my way of giving back to God, by loving the people whom He lavishly loves, letting them know about His power to set them free, and His faithfulness to empower them to live life more abundantly.

I started health and wellness transformation coaching entrepreneurship because being a highly sensitive person, I see and feel people's suffering and pain. Witnessing struggles in healthcare for more than thirty years, my heart breaks for people desperate for healing. So many people are disheartened and feel lost after going to different doctors, services, and specialties. Healthcare, which is more geared towards physical health or acute health issues, fails to address the whole person. Even with technological advancement and sincere efforts to collaborate, care can be fragmented. People who have health issues go to one doctor who usually runs some tests and prescribes a pill. Then the patient either gets more pills or gets referred to another specialist until they keep adding to the list of medications and their side effects. We need more than that. We need compassionate caregivers who will spend time listening and answering their questions. They need advocates, people who would care for what matters to them, support them, and fight for their rights. I wanted to be that person, not because I wanted to be a hero, but because I wanted to be Christ's representative to the hurting and broken, and let them experience His salvation, healing, and faithfulness. I also wanted to equip others to do the same and God honored that desire.

As a nurse, case manager, and coach, I have helped hundreds of patients and clients with their physical, emotional, mental, spiritual, and relational health. I am grateful that when we depend on the Holy Spirit, He reveals to us and empowers us to help people heal. If we sincerely want others to find healing and restoration, we have to value and take care of the whole person. Something that is lacking in our current traditional healthcare. I want to be obedient to God and be used by him to fill that gap. I want others to know that they too can overcome adversities and become victorious in this life!

The world needs authentic, transformative coaches because it is hard to navigate life on our own. We need coaches who would lead people back to God, so they can discover their true identity and God-given gifts and purpose. It has been said that the grave is the richest place on earth. Why? because so many people die and get buried with their gifts, talents, and dreams still inside of them. I don't want that to happen to me or anyone I know. Instead, I want to pour them out to make a difference and a lasting impact in people's lives, for God's glory and honor.

People often tell me they believe it's not an accident they are talking to me and sharing their deepest hurts. They wonder why they feel like they finally found someone they can trust, and that it's safe to share. This is because when the Holy Spirit tells me to meet with or call someone, I pray for them beforehand, and even when I don't know what to say, the Holy Spirit shows up, supplies the words, and ministers to them through me.

The same is true when I pray for people. I allow and invite the Holy Spirit to lead and minister to the person I'm praying for, then they experience clarity and wisdom that helps them move forward. I will always be grateful for having these, that others consider hard or difficult. I consider them opportunities to allow God to do what Only He can do.

As Christ's followers, we have been given discernment. We know God is being pushed out of schools, businesses, and the marketplace. Why? because of people's agenda and greed. The devil knows when people experience Jesus, they will experience fulfillment and freedom, and it would be hard to manipulate them to believe his lies. The devil wants to bring chaos, and he uses all kinds of tactics to distract people, so they won't have time to communicate and connect with God to know the power that is within them when they accept Christ as Lord and Savior.

I believe a Kingdom business stands out because it's aligned with God's Word. Furthermore, it follows the most important principles in the Bible. Matthew 6:33 says, "But seek Ye first, the Kingdom of God, and His righteousness, and all these things else will be added unto you" (KJV). Living by and practicing Kingdom principles in your profession and business makes a difference in such a way that people know you care for them sincerely. They respond and get results because they first know they can trust you; when they know you believe in them, they start believing in themselves and their abilities to change and move forward.

Have you considered incorporating obedience to God in your business? What is God asking of you? Where is He directing you?

When the people you serve know that you value them and they can relate to you because you've been where they are, they start to pay attention. They want to partner with you in their journey, and in the process find hope and inspiration, and later experience restoration, healing, and transformation. Transformation efforts may be well-meaning, but without God, it is constrained, short-term, and is bound to fail. A Kingdom business stands out because it is rooted in love and service! Its main purpose is to help and empower people. It is based on biblical principles, so it focuses on impact and purpose more than financial benefits. It goes back to reverence and obedience to God!

Blessings and favor come as a result of obedience. When I practice obedience, God directs my steps and puts everything in order: my life, my health, and my family.

I remember when we were still in the Philippines, and I didn't have a job after raising my daughters. I heard God say to serve and use my gifts where I am. I served in a church by teaching and mentoring young adults. Not long after, I got an offer to work at a hospital, then immigrate here in the United

States as a Nurse, and our lives have never been the same since. I have been blessed to have the privilege of helping and empowering patients in various areas of nursing: in hospitals, clinics, and nursing homes. We also received many blessings in our health, finances, relationships, and material blessings. We are so blessed to be able to buy a beautiful home with a view of the lake and mountains, nice cars, and everything we need. Another blessing we're grateful for is that we were able to send both kids to the University of Washington, where they completed their degrees in public health, and are now using their gifts and skills to serve others.

OBEDIENCE AS A KINGDOM PRINCIPLE

Kingdom principles are important because they guide our values and help define our identity. They help translate our purpose and mission and guide our decisions and actions. This book enumerates some of them. I chose obedience because I believe this is central to the Christian walk. Obedience is an act of worship. It is what is necessary to live this life freely and abundantly. It brings us freedom, peace, joy, and prosperity. Obedience produces favor and blessings. It is the key that unlocks God's promises.

When God created us, He provided everything we needed. He sent His son, Jesus, so we can connect with Him and have a model for how to live life on Earth. Jesus is the first and greatest example of what obedience to the Father looks like. He willingly gave up His position in Heaven, and obeyed the Father, even to the point of suffering a gruesome death to save us from our sins. Now He is seated at the right hand of God and all authority is given to Him.

Aside from Jesus, the Bible is filled with many stories of obedience. Moses obeyed when God asked him to talk to Pharaoh to free His people from slavery and take them on the journey to the promised land. Abraham, in obedience to God, took His son, Isaac, to be sacrificed as a burnt offering, and because Abraham feared and obeyed God, He provided a ram to be sacrificed instead. Noah built an ark, even when there were no signs of rain, but because He heard from God and obeyed, his whole household was saved from the flood.

Although our motivation is not just so we would receive blessings, I have found that when we love and obey God, He honors our desire to obey Him. I have examples of these in my life. Growing up in poverty, God provided for my needs, healed my diseases, and gave me opportunities for learning and improving myself. As I entered the workforce, I would apply for jobs others thought I was not qualified to hold. Not believing people's opinions of

OBEDIENCE PRODUCES BLESSINGS

me, I was hired for positions that people would have never guessed I would get. I have since pioneered and implemented pilot transformation projects in healthcare. I have learned that when we obey God and align our thoughts and actions with His will and His Word, He honors our obedience, blesses us, and gives us unmerited favor!

WHAT DOES OBEDIENCE LOOK LIKE FOR US?

"Now that you have purified yourselves, by obeying the truth, so that you have sincere love for each other, love one another deeply, from the heart!" -1 Peter 1:22, NIV

First, let's define what it's not. Obedience is not about following what God says because we are after the rewards or what He can do for us. We obey because we know without a shadow of a doubt that He is faithful and trustworthy, not because we were told by others, or are afraid He is going to punish us if we don't do as He pleases. That is what religion does. Obedience is about a relationship with Jesus. Obedience is listening to God, doing what He asks us to do, and going where He's calling us to go, even when it's hard, or it doesn't make sense. Obeying Him means we trust that the Father has given Him authority; it means we revere Him and put Him in the highest regard, as the King of Kings and Lord of Lords. We obey Him because we love Him, we want to honor and emulate Him! It's about loving people who are sometimes difficult, or who others might call unlovable.

Obedience is attached to wisdom. It's about diligently seeking His face, being still, and listening to the heart of God. It's taking the first step and trusting that He will do as He promised!

OBEDIENCE IN BUSINESS:

While everyone else is obsessed with making wealth, obedience to God means loving and serving people first, and trusting God for what He does, and multiplies!

I choose to wait on God's timing and for His download. This happens when I intentionally let go of distractions and spend purposeful and dedicated time focusing on His presence and listening to what He wants to say. This usually happens when I'm outdoors enjoying nature, worshiping, in my dreams, or ministering to people. It's not always easy to trust and patiently wait, but I believe He owns it all, and He rewards those whom He loves and whose trust is in Him!

Entrepreneurship is a way of serving and empowering people by using our gifts and talents to make God known and give Him glory and honor.

Wealth belongs to God, and He gave us the ability to co-create it on earth, as it is in heaven. He blesses the work of our hands when we stick to the values and do it in obedience. Through our businesses, we impact the world, by doing it with love and compassion. After all, our main motivation is to truly and sincerely help others become the best version of themselves, the way God created and called them to be.

Obedience to God is the opposite of what our society teaches. We live in an upside-down world, and that is why it is not easy to obey God and His Word, especially if we listen to other's opinions, the voices in our heads, and how we feel. This is also why relationships are broken and businesses fail. Obedience is something that is freely given and not forced. To obey God, we will give up the strong need to be right, to be first. Instead of going after what we think is right in our own eyes, or what would make us get ahead in life, Jesus gave us examples in the Bible of how to be obedient to the Father and serve with humility! To practice obedience in our lives and businesses, we should have His commandments as a foundation. He commanded us to love Him with all our minds, hearts, and souls, and the second commandment is to love our neighbors as ourselves. This is the foundation that would guide us on how we operate our lives and our businesses. How we run our business and treat people shows our obedience to God.

KINGDOM BUSINESS TIPS AND STRATEGIES:

1. Seek God, ask for direction, and thank Him for your gifts, talents, and opportunities. Surrender your heart to Jesus and ask for the Holy Spirit's leading and direction. Abide in Christ by meditating on His Word, let this be your source of truth.
2. Align your mission, vision, and values to His Word. Obey what God is asking you to do, even when it doesn't make sense. When problems arise, pause, pray, and praise!
3. Value people and build them up. Praise and reward them generously. Listen to them, make them feel heard, and known. Serve your people, and do not ever take advantage of anyone.
4. Be generous. Serve using 4 E's daily: encourage, engage, empower, and equip your people.
5. Practice great customer service. Overdeliver in your promises.
6. As your business grows, check your motivation often. Your action depends on it.

Lastly, freedom and fulfillment come when we are obedient and in alignment with God's plan in our lives. We've seen many wealthy and famous people who are unhappy and dissatisfied with life. We all know celebrities who are prosperous in the world's eye view but end up depressed and taking their own lives. This tells us that things or riches alone would not satisfy. When we don't find purpose and meaning in what we do, everything is meaningless, as Solomon, the wisest man ever alive says in the Old Testament of the Bible.

When I was still working at the hospital, I was so affected by what happens to patients when their health gets compromised. Being highly sensitive, I could feel their pain, their anguish, their unmet needs. With my experience and discernment, I could almost see how their condition would end. I prayed for miracles. I prayed that God would show me how I can truly help people so they don't suffer. God opened my eyes and let me know I did not become a nurse just to follow orders, give medications, or make them comfortable when I am with them. I can teach and empower people to take care of their health and prevent disease. The result has been phenomenal. The people whose lives were forever changed, and who have been able to meet their health goals is a testament to God's favor. We can always make plans on our own, but in the end, it's God's will that makes things happen. Our knowledge, skills, and experiences alone are not enough. We need to submit them to God and listen for His ideas, strategies, and downloads. We need a true relationship with God, and the discipline to listen, trust, and obey God if we want to be victorious and successful in this life, and in our Kingdom business. When our relationship with Jesus is central to everything we do, we believe our main purpose is to obey and glorify God, and our actions will be in alignment with our goals, and His plans for us.

I pray we trust and obey Him in every stage, and every season, in our lives, and our businesses.

ABOUT THE AUTHOR

Evangeline is a nationally board-certified health and wellness coach, a certified coach, speaker, trainer, parenting and family coach from the John Maxwell Team, and a certified health coach from the Institute of Integrative Nutrition. She has a certificate for mental health coaching from Light University. She graduated with a bachelor's in nursing from Far Eastern University and currently works as a Whole Health RN and Network Wide Education Faculty in Seattle, Washington. As an RN, she has served patients in OB-GYN, Pediatrics, Medical Surgical, Transplant, ICU Stepdown, Neuroscience, Epilepsy, and Stroke Units. She has also served as Director of Staff Development for a nursing home in Westland, Michigan. She has implemented three transformation grant projects in health care, namely, Primary Care Transformation, Transforming Clinical Practice Initiative, and Whole Health.

She is passionate about serving, inspiring, and helping people heal, reach their goals, and live a joyful, meaningful, and victorious life. She is dedicated to equipping, mentoring, and empowering others in their journey to holistic healing, and finding their highest calling. She loves meeting people where they are, sharing about God, her experiences, challenges, and how she found grace, hope, and freedom in Christ. During her free time, she loves spending time with family, reading books, cooking, gardening, listening to music, playing with her dogs, Milo and Koko, and hiking with her husband of 27 years, Ernest, and daughters Kathleen and Vanessa. talented young women, both from the University of Washington.

To Connect with Evangeline:

Email: mailto:evangelinecoach@gmail.com
Website: https://www.evangelinepescasio.com

Other Books:

Restored: Hope and Healing for the Lost and Broken
Restored: Hope and Healing for the Lost and Broken Workbook

CHAPTER 4

Stewardship - A Message for You

Lorraine Woods, USA
ARTIST

Angry and frustrated, I was not feeling or seeing God's love and provisions in my life. This stemmed from not knowing who I was; subsequently, I did not manage any area in my life in partnership with God. Biblical stewardship is the utilization of Kingdom principles by someone who manages God's Kingdom here on Earth and it begins with each individual; it's my choice. That option was non-existent while growing up. I did not know who I was. From early childhood, I was compared to others, which led to trying different personalities so I could fit in - somewhere. This all fell apart many years later when the mask I had worn since early childhood dropped -

Stewardship - A Message for You

leaving me unable to work. Like Humpty Dumpty who fell off the wall, I was fragmented into pieces within myself - unable to proceed in my life. The deep wound in my soul rendered me incapable of working any longer. Nearly twenty-nine years strung together in cycles of working and quitting, mostly as a Certified Nursing Assistant, had come to an end. I had "flatlined" from a life of mental, verbal, emotional, and physical abuse in both my home growing up and later in marriage and was placed on prescribed antidepressants. I did not know what I liked or didn't like. I truly was a blank page. I never thought this would happen to me. I did everything I knew to do, including listening to messages and reading the Bible and other books advised by church leaders. Before the 2006 crash, I was hungry to know more about Jesus and the Holy Spirit as opposed to religion.

Growing up, I went to church but did not know what was said as it was in Latin and I drifted through life, until years later, when I had my Pentecostal encounter. I was in church every time the doors were open, attending classes and water baptized as rededication, yet my life would eventually fall apart. It was as though the lights had gone out. Where was God? What did I do wrong? I was alone in all of this and afraid.

February 2006 brought in a stormy wind of change intended to impact both the church and the world. The "storms" inside during this time reminded me of a scene from the movie *The Wizard of Oz* when Dorothy experienced the winds blowing, moving her life, but the difference is I wasn't going to wake up from a bad dream. This bad dream continued as reports from ministries testified of praying for healing and recovery for people and were alarmed at the opposite results. I believed I was somehow the cause of these losses; the generational roots of guilt, accusations, and rejection were there before I was born. This mental and emotional storm played a role in the crack in my old foundation, which shattered in pieces, and I had desperation for Jesus in a way I had never experienced before. Kingdom management over my life began in a new way. I could hear the voice of the Holy Spirit with greater clarity than before and I began writing notes and highlighting passages of scriptures with dates included to help keep a timeline as my journey began.

Just as Jacob in the Old Testament had his encounter with "the God of his fathers", I was suddenly on my journey with Him too. It was no longer "my mother's religion," but an intimate relationship with scriptures and the Holy Spirit. Like Jacob partnering with God resulted in the multiplication of his livestock, journaling revelations, understandings, and promises the Holy Spirit gave me resulted in the increase of my art production and commissions. Ideas and strategies come to me just as they did for Jacob with the branches to multiply his livestock. We can hear His Voice and follow His directions: "My sheep hear My Voice, I know them, and they follow Me" (John 10:27, NKJV)

Identity gives us purpose as is exemplified by Jacob in the Old Testament. As he was destined with his legacy, we as Kingdom artisans also have a legacy to leave to our posterity, be it through our family line, or spiritual family. Revelation of His righteousness shifted something in me that February day and the old sinful me was exposed with a great awareness of the need for the blood sacrifice of Christ. I needed to love myself first so I could bring this to others. Eventually, I understood it was a message for everyone.

The gifts I had suppressed suddenly came forward. Creative giftings and other assets that were overlooked in my life growing up, now are utilized in helping other women discover their identities a loving God has given them. Through my relationship, I could hear the Spirit of Christ and I understood I was to bring my gifts to others to help heal and rebuild our lives including income.

Unlike the world's system, the work I do brings inspiration and creativity given by and acknowledging our Creator and will heal areas in our lives because of the exchange of our *old* selves for the *new* Kingdom Identity. The exchange of the finished work of the cross Jesus suffered, and His resurrection gives us His identity (for those who believe in their hearts). A new message is assigned to each of us to impact lives to bring vision and purpose to others and to help those of us who are not generating income from our art gifts.

As Kingdom creatives, we can inspire individual lives impacting the arts industry. It also affects families as hobbies, homeschoolers, family nights at the movies, and book reading become a healing and nurturing force in itself.

It was in my teen years I began making oil paintings which were commissioned by relatives, and some sold at the local art festival. The Internet was non-existent, and I realized I didn't know anything about business and marketing. What was branding? What was my niche? I wasn't recognized for any particular genre or theme. I would look at the works of various artists and experiment at home but never achieved authority of my own.

My unsold collection appeared as pieces collected from various artists because I had no identity and as a new artist, I was trying to fit in somewhere. I didn't have my own style. My artwork reflected that fragmentation resulting in disjointed random art pieces. My artmaking was therapy for me. While other artists mastered their genre, themes, or branding, I didn't and hid behind my talent: no branding, no following. No marketing so people didn't know I existed! The private painting classes I paid for didn't include marketing practices other than business cards and buying a fax machine. Emails didn't exist and competition was high in artist circles. I was always at the student level. I would watch the work of other artists sell and question, *"Why not mine?"* I would try different subjects and never grow in my subject skills or knowledge. The talent was there and skills were being built, but I had no knowledge of what I needed to think about. Client follow-up, branding my work, knowledge of mediums, resources, and expansion of a theme or a message didn't exist in my small studio world.

    This all changed for me later in my life after my losses in divorce. It felt like I'd been stripped bare of everything I had and knew. I was fully aware of who I was and my need for my Creator had me desperate for His guidance. He was real and I was at a new start in my life. I now had a purpose that changed every area of my life including my art! I had a message to bring to others! The Holy Spirit is real and wants to partner with and talk to us. He empowers us to live out the lives we were intended to live. The first change I noticed was in my art which reflected the change inside. My work was more brilliant with color choices than in my past, yet I was prompted by the Holy Ghost to draw stick figures as visuals one time while speaking in a church meeting where people were encouraged to bring a word or message. I was obedient to do this (although afraid), and people were impacted. My message at this meeting was the new thing God was doing. A move of the Holy Ghost sparked the pastor to bring up anointing oil and people went up for prayer. The drawing wasn't anything special, it was obedience to a prompting God had already planned before I got there. Obedience is key.

My message was about the new thing God was doing and how critical it is to renew our minds. My stick figures were simple visuals for greater impact that enhanced the words of my message, and it worked! A couple of men shifted in their thinking (and who knows how many others I wasn't aware of) because of my obedience. This was confirmation of the start of a movement, but I didn't think of it that way; I only knew I needed to be obedient. A few years later, I was obedient to mailing out portraits in my country to families who lost loved ones to violence in tragic circumstances. I knew I needed to do this; I was a part of God's hand of healing that was started in my homeland. "When the enemy comes in like a flood, the Spirit of the Lord will lift a standard against him" (Isaiah 59:19, NKJV). It was no longer a pretty painting to hang on a wall. This was changing how I thought of what I was doing and why. It was noticed by leaders in a couple of countries. His Kingdom come.

Stewarding my self-care is a part of the healing process. Why the healing process? We "may prosper in all things and be in health, just as your soul prospers" (3 John 2, NKJV). My understanding is that if I steward my choices of diet, relationships, and what I listen to, I can expect healthy or healthier living. Even my relationship with money was neglected growing up. Coming from a comfortable upbringing, I never figured out I needed wisdom to manage my finances. Dad was always there to help bail me out. Also, I had emotional and mental issues (generational curses) on both sides of the family. Generational curses can be recognized by such things as emotional and/or mental illnesses, addictions, domestic violence, multiple partners or divorces, obesity from poor diets, birth defects, or health conditions, to name some. A number of these occur in family members or generations and it becomes frustrating when all efforts out of this don't appear to help. Breakthrough can bring freedom and I can attest to this!

Learning to forgive yourself as Jesus forgives you is a part of stewarding from a healed heart. Your creative processes produce work your audience engages in; something you do no one else can, and others who want art with your style. Loving yourself so we can love others is obedience, and blessing follows because our thinking shifts. If our thinking changes to how God thinks, we too make changes in decisions and become a part of bringing the Kingdom here. We're more important than a sparrow or a flower Jesus tells us. This means we align ourselves to receive God's goodness.

"Keep yourselves in the love of God, looking for the mercy of our Lord Jesus Christ unto eternal life." - Jude 1:21, NKJV

Coasting through my life without purpose or direction, I had nothing to give or aspire to, while my friends were going to business or nursing schools and marrying. I made art. I attended four years in a school of design. During my junior year portfolio critique by the faculty, I felt silly playing with colors when I wanted to join the Peace Corps or Vista to help oppressed people. God would have His way in this life eventually, and my faith is married to art to

STEWARDSHIP - A MESSAGE FOR YOU

inspire and encourage other women. A first generation of a Charismatic encounter, I put into practice what I was hearing from the pulpit and reading from my Bible but investing it into a toxic marriage. God honored this as my roots drove deeper into my spiritual convictions and tethered me in my faith for what was coming. I took my faith, Bible, and art supplies with me into an unknown future when my marriage ended. A new compassion for people arose in me in 2006 and God was forming in me a message for today. If you have read this far, this message is for you. My first understanding of God's identity in me, and what the purpose of my very existence is, helped me after losing everything when my marriage came to an end. Who He is in me and what that means changed how I thought. I wanted to hand the reins over to my Creator. Vulnerability replaced independence and I connected with the women at church at a level I never experienced previously. New relationships were a gift and I understood I needed to prioritize them. My first portrait sketch came forward in a new sister-in-Christ friendship who mentored me for a short time before she moved. This relational-independent, isolated artist was now a part of a community. God is about family.

The first step to managing creativity in your business is to always begin with the directive from Matthew 6:33, "But seek first the kingdom of God and His righteousness, and all these things will be added to you" (NKJV). Put God first. He owns everything anyway. Manage everything He gives you, and He will add what you need as you partner with Him. What does a partnership with God mean? Invite Him into all your determinations and yield to His guidance. Going for walks on the trails or sitting at the beach has an inspiring effect on many artists. Alternating between creating art and scripture reading is always a joyful experience for me as I add divine character traits in my work.

Trust and obedience ushers in the next level of willingness to "color outside the lines" through challenges, as God meets you at the next step forward. What does this look like? I push myself to intentionally love His Word and actively do something relevant to my message despite my circumstances that may oppose my ability to do something. I don't wait until my financial circumstances change; I find something to sketch on. It may be the flip side of a painting on paper and posting on social media. This recently happened and two people were interested in buying those pieces even though the papers were buckled from water.

Stewardship - A Message for You

I trusted God; He honors faith and obedience as we act upon the prompting inside us.

Start now; don't wait until you have all the materials and resources to begin. If you have begun at any level, don't procrastinate in doing something new for lack of materials or resources. This can be the best time to get creative or connect with people socially. For artists and anyone working from home, life can be isolating in the studio or home office, so I go to my favorite coffee shops and ask strangers for feedback on my book illustrations. People love art and feel like they have something valuable to share. I have made friends by doing this which subsequently generated interest in my work. It's important to have authority in your field and to experiment with name brands and mediums. Confidence in your product builds a strong portfolio and favor, and doors of opportunities do open.

Know yourself and what environment and atmosphere work to your benefit. Pray over your work and for your audience. God is the Creator and knows what you need. Humility is a door opener; the only one to compete with is yourself. Esteem another business owner - it's amazing how much joy is released, and freedom comes in which, in turn, affects your relationships and decisions that were difficult previously.

I incorporate business decisions as I work. For example, I once was commissioned to paint someone's four cats. Instead of holding my brain processes back to each portrait and unique colors and markings, I took a photo of all four in their beginning stage, incorporated marketing techniques, and posted it on social media asking people how they would proceed with this. When done, I worked on each so they all had colors started. I was immediately satisfied with how quickly this big project was finishing. My brain was increasing in its capacity to think beyond one piece and into multiples. A macro-mindset is being cultivated and comes after the initial skills you develop. Set boundaries within yourself. Dr. Henry Cloud's book *Changes That Heal* is a good read that applies to whatever you are facing. Heart posture is first for relationships and is essential in your foundation to hear God. He will guide your steps if you listen. Receive God's love and forgiveness. Forgive and love yourself and love others. Keep joy because that is your strength.

"Seek first the Kingdom of God and His righteousness and all these things will be added to you." - Matthew 6:33, NKJV

ABOUT THE AUTHOR

Lorraine Woods attended the Swain School of Design in New Bedford, MA., UMass Dartmouth in North Dartmouth, MA., and holds a B.F.A. She has exhibited in art festivals and taught private and group Art classes for adults and children. Lorraine works with various mediums with her favorite being pastels. She is a children's book author and illustrator and hopes to lead children to authorship. Lorraine's life experiences began with a crayon in early childhood; various, unexpected people noted the talent and encouraged the gift. God is Faithful.

Lorraine is a Mom to an adult son and lives in Georgia, USA.

To Connect with Lorraine:

Email: woodslor@yahoo.com
    (List ARTWORK as the subject)

Facebook: Lorraine Woods Artist

CHAPTER 5

Stewardship

Lenora Stone, USA
PROPHETIC GRAPHIC DESIGNER

THE STORY BEHIND CHAMPIONING THE CHAMPIONS

Championing The Champions was formed after I had a prophetic dream in which I was branding Kingdom entrepreneurs. I was partnering with Heaven to create a visual identity for those God had called into the marketplace. Before this encounter, the Holy Spirit had been speaking to me about a wealth transfer (as in Proverbs 13:22) and Kingdom entrepreneurs entering the marketplace to advance the gospel. When I prayed into the dream, the Lord helped me develop a framework for prophetic branding and design. As the Lord is calling His people

STEWARDSHIP

into the marketplace as His reformers, He is inviting each of us to upgrade into the fullness of our call that is attached to the great end-times harvest. He created us for global impact! In addition to branding with Heaven's vision, the Lord put on my heart to offer prophetic business consultations, intercession, and inner healing as part of equipping His entrepreneurs for their next level. This process of brand development is twofold in the sense that God develops both the vision and the Champion(s) who carry the vision throughout the branding experience. This process is called *visioneering.* Often during this time, the Lord will give downloads and blueprints for clients to see the way Heaven sees them and to engage with that vision for their lives. We then partner with Heaven to build for the now with scaling to the larger vision in mind during that development process. This revelation of visioneering brought clarity to my journey because my career before design was in career coaching, family counseling, and inner healing. When I sought God's vision for Championing The Champions, He spoke to me about equipping and unveiling His remnant. The remnant is His end-times army – the saints who are wholeheartedly dedicated to advancing the Gospel and preparing the way for the return of Christ.

Championing The Champions goes beyond branding. Prophetic consultations and intercession cast vision and break open the way for clients to walk fully in the purpose and identity God wrote when He created them. After seeking His heart, I have worked diligently to create a space where Holy Spirit-led design, intercession, prophetic strategy, and Kingdom community would equip His entrepreneurs to fulfill their purpose on earth. How do we bring Heaven to earth? This will happen as we each allow Heaven to brand and equip us to stand in our identity and call. As we fully engage our purpose and champion one another in unity, we will reform our nation and all the nations on Earth. As Kingdom Entrepreneurs, our branding and business ideas should be a step above the rest because we have the counsel of Heaven. God is our CEO and we co-labor with Him as we enter into the marketplace and the world.

What Sets Championing The Champions Apart

When clients work with Championing The Champions, we seek the vision and strategy of Heaven together. Often when launching or scaling a business intercession is required. Championing The Champions isn't just a place where clients receive strategy and design; it is also a launching place. It is a place where God-ideas, callings, and community can develop in partnership with the Lord. There

Stewardship

is intercessory coverage, encouragement, accountability, equipping, and community which is necessary to overcome the warfare that comes along with promotion. Prophetic consultations provide insight for branding and design, but they also equip clients with what they need to move forward in the specific call and identity God has for them in their next season. Inner work is key to outer success. The Lord has impressed upon me Championing the Champions is a consultation-driven business. I'm not just a designer or simply a prophetic designer – but one who truly champions clients and seeks the vision of Heaven for clients professionally and personally. This brings an elevation and breakthrough beyond what branding alone can do. If you are a Kingdom Entrepreneur, imagine the incredible strategy and elevation that can come from partnering with a prophetic designer. When we submit the designs and business ideas to the Lord, our CEO, He gives the wisdom to build businesses and clients upon the solid rock because it is the Lord who is building the business. It brings an alignment and positioning above the rest. It also brings an increased trust in the Lord to launch and steward God-ideas and unlocks the faith to not only dream wildly with Him but to steward those dreams and see them in reality!

Stewarding God's Call On Our Lives

In the next few sections, I'm going to share with you some keys and prophetic activations for going to your next level and then going from victory to victory!

Last year God asked me to attend a conference for intercessors with Jennifer LeClaire. She spoke about stewardship and multiplication. The theme of the conference was 100x multiplication with God. Before I left, the Lord had me reading the parable of the talents. For reference, a talent most often represents provision, but can also apply to actual talents and gifts from God. There is so much depth in this passage. Three people who receive talents from their Master are expected to steward them well by multiplying them before He returns. The person who received one talent buried the talent he received out of fear of losing it. The one who received two talents doubled it. And the one who received five talents also doubled their portion. The one who buried his talent was counted as evil and lazy. The Master took his one talent and gave it to the one who stewarded the most talents well. The scripture following this parable is Matthew 25:29, "To those who use well what they are given, even more will be given, and they will have an abundance. But from those who do nothing, even what little they have will be taken away." (NLT).

Stewardship

This scripture shows the importance of stewarding well what God has given us. There is a reason each of us is here on the earth. We each have a specific unique call and assignment from the Lord to steward and advance His plans on the earth. Just like the passage in 1 Corinthians 12 when Paul speaks of the different parts of the Body of Christ. Each part is needed for the full body to work together for His greater purpose. This also applies to entrepreneurship and ministry. The reformation of the marketplace and bringing God's Kingdom to the earth will take an army of Kingdom influencers fully embracing their call and stewarding the gifts God has placed within them. You were created for such a time as this!

Activation: Dreaming With God

Now is the time to begin to seek God's heart for your purpose and how to steward the gifts He has given you. It's time to dream audacious dreams with God! I challenge you to ask Him today, *"What are You dreaming about right now for me? How can I believe You for the more (as in Ephesians 3:20)?"* Another question you can ask is *"Lord, are there any million or billion-dollar ideas you want to share with me to steward to advance your Kingdom?"* Journal His response. Take time to put some soaking music on or worship until you feel His Presence. Then ask Him to share His heart with you. This is part of building in the Glory rather than on our own. Ruth Heflin, David Hertzog, and Joshua Mills are valuable resources on building with God in the Glory. Once you feel God's Presence, ask Him if there is anything you have set down or buried He desires for you to pick back up again. Are there any prophetic words or promises He wants to remind you of? Write down anything He highlights. Repent for any ways you have buried talents, dreams, or ideas He has asked you to steward. Then ask Him for your next step(s). As you step out in faith and obedience to do your part, God will unveil more steps and provide the miracles for God dreams to become a reality.

Community Is Key For Sustained Victory

When Nehemiah rebuilt the walls, He did not do it alone. The book of Nehemiah has many valuable lessons for building with God. When we put our hand to the plow and build with God, it's also important to seek Him for the community we are called to build with. God-led community and unity are key to sustained revival. God's plans for our lives are greater than anything we can do on our own. In the Kingdom of God, competition is eliminated and replaced with collaboration. When we understand each person has a unique call and is created to function together to bring God's Kingdom to the earth; the understanding of championing one

Stewardship

another is unlocked. This is part of the reason for the name Championing The Champions. We are each champions championing other champions in fulfilling the mandate of the Great Commission to, "go into all the world and preach the Gospel to all creation" (Mark 16:15, NKJV).

Activation: Building With Your Covenant People

Proverbs 27:17 says, "As iron sharpens iron, so one person sharpens another" (NIV). Ask the Holy Spirit, *"Who do you want me to partner with to build the dreams you have given me? Is there a training or community I need to be a part of to grow into the person you've called me to be?"* Oftentimes, there are leaders and communities the Lord will direct you to partner with to be equipped in your call. A corporate anointing of prayer and worship will accelerate your call far more than doing it on your own. There are coaches and leaders who can call out the excellence in you, hold you accountable, and teach you to avoid pitfalls. Their seasoned wisdom and victory are imparted to you, so you don't have to learn the hard way.

Additionally, there are people you are meant to build with. Their gifts and calls align with yours–sometimes for a season, and sometimes for life. God will highlight them as your covenant people to build

His Kingdom with. Partnering with them will advance you both in those God-given dreams and advance the Kingdom powerfully!

God Ideas Come In Seed Form

Years ago, I had a vision about stewarding multiple prophetic births. He was revealing we are in a time where multiple prophetic births are occurring simultaneously throughout the earth. He is equipping His bride for mass intergenerational revival. The Holy Spirit showed me the importance of being trustworthy and equipped to remain in the birthing room. Prophetic consultations are often a place where the Holy Spirit uses me and others to yield to Him as a midwife to facilitate prophetic births and nurture promises after the birth. Similar to births in the natural – each birth is unique. Some are quiet and calm, and some are loud and messy. Some come with ease, and some are painful. Some happen alone and others happen in public places. He showed me that, just like in life, birth is the beginning. We have to nurture and steward what He births through us to grow it in full fruition and maturity. This maturity allows those prophetic promises to have the impact He desires. The prophetic word, the God idea, or revelation of those promises is like conception. Declaring the promise out in intercession and preparation is like pregnancy. Part of stewardship is stewarding prophetic words well.

Through prophetic training, I've learned prophetic words aren't something we receive then put on a shelf waiting for them to happen. Instead, they are an invitation from the Lord to engage those words. We do our part, and He does His. It's a partnership with Heaven. There is a relational component to it. It draws us closer to God. The more we seek Him concerning prophetic words we have received, tested, and acted on, the more He reveals the blueprint on how to steward it. Just like how the development of film on vintage cameras takes time to process and slowly reveals an image as the process is carried out, this is how prophetic words develop. As we pray, seek wise counsel, and take action steps in obedience, the prophetic words become more clear. More revelation and action steps come as we steward what we have received. Each step builds upon the other. Prophetic promises come in seed form. Just like a farmer prepares the ground, nurtures the seeds and plants, and then harvests them; the Lord expects us to do the same. It is a constant and continual relationship, and the beautiful way God brings Heaven to Earth through us.

Activation: Cultivating Prophetic Promises

Take time to ask the Lord: *"Are there any prophetic words I have forgotten or put on the shelf?"* Ask Him to highlight a prophetic word to you with one action step to engage it. Take the action step He gives and be expectant for fulfilled promises.

If you have not received a prophetic word, take time to sit with the Lord and ask Him to reveal His heart for you. Ask Him what He wants you to know to step into who you are called to be! Reflect on the following passage and let your heart be encouraged that the Lord has amazing plans for your life and wants to share them with you. In Jeremiah 29:11-13 it says, "For I know the thoughts that I think toward you,' says the Lord, 'thoughts of peace and not of evil, to give you a future and a hope. Then you will call upon Me and go and pray to Me, and I will listen to you. And you will seek Me and find Me, when you search for Me with all your heart" (NKJV).

Cultivating Systems & Disciplines

Back to the intercessor's conference: something I admire about Jennifer LeClaire is how she models good stewardship. One way that impacted me significantly is waking up at 3:30 a.m. every day to pray and work. Her dedication to stewardship for the Kingdom of God inspired me to develop my schedule for better stewardship. Later I heard this is a habit of

STEWARDSHIP

millionaires and billionaires. They get their most focused work done in the morning while most people are sleeping. The conference taught me so much about good stewardship and laid a foundation for me to learn to go to the next level. I began asking, *"Lord, how can I be a good steward? What systems and habits do I need to set up to fully walk out my call? What changes do I need to make to steward the gifts You have given with excellence? Who do I need to invite into my life for accountability and discipleship? What do I need to learn? Lord, make me a good steward who receives the more You described in Ephesians 3:20. Help me raise good stewards by sharing what You have taught me."*

An incredible book the Lord used in my life to develop stewardship is *Atomic Habits* by James Clear. In this book, he encourages readers to build habits by envisioning what the person they want to become would do. We can take this a step further with the prophetic. Part of engaging the vision God has shared over our lives is turning our prophetic words into decrees and action steps. Take the vision *He has given you and ask yourself how does one with this call live? What habits, routines, and thoughts do they have? How do they treat their family, others, and self? On a practical level, what does one with this call wear? How does the Lord want to dress you and display you in this season?* When we engage Heaven's vision in this practical action-oriented way, it transforms us into the likeness of Christ and equips us in the fullness of our calls.

Activation: Systems & Disciplines

I encourage you to ask the Lord the same questions for your life. Let's become good stewards together! Ask the Lord to reveal who He has called you to be and write His answers down.

The next step is to write decrees from what He reveals. Throughout each day partner with God's vision for your life by declaring who He says you are and what He has promised as though it is already so. As a parent or grandparent, you can do this for your children and grandchildren! You could voice record the decrees and promises filling your heart and mind with God's promises for your life by listening and declaring them every day. This will activate His promises, build your faith, and show good stewardship. This action brings Heaven's vision to earth through faith. James 2:26 says, "Faith without works is dead" (NKJV).

The third part of this is seeking God's heart for wisdom and revelation as well as practical knowledge on how to create, refine, and keep habits, systems, and disciplines to take you to the next level. Ask yourself what the *future you* would do and start implementing those habits today to see the fruit of what Heaven is saying over your life! Implement what the Lord is sharing even if it is challenging and out of your current routine or comfort zone. His wisdom makes our path straight and brings abundant life!

HEALING FOUNDATIONS

Before God promotes us, He deals with our foundations. Because of His love for us, He brings healing and deliverance to places of brokenness. His truth shatters the lies that hold us back and His safe love empowers us to confront those places that hinder us from walking in the fullness of our call and in the complete inheritance Jesus paid the price for. We are commanded to walk in unity because as the Body of Christ, we function together as one body to build and enforce the Kingdom of God on Earth. Unhealed wounds leave room for the enemy and can hinder our ability to stay unified and unoffendable. The Lord does not want wounded warriors to stay wounded. He wants to heal His beloved and raise up healed warriors who walk fully in their call and have the capacity to bring His healing to others. When we have unhealed areas, it creates a cap and limits how far we can go. It impacts our ability to clearly see, hear from God, and translate His messages to others. To experience breakthroughs such as family restoration, thriving businesses, fulfilled promises, and beyond that both national and international revival; we must be diligent in seeking God's heart and obeying the steps He asks us to take for healing and deliverance. It's not just about building, but also about allowing Him to tear down anything not of Him and rebuild everything that is of Him in our lives. To be trusted with more and walk out our call successfully, we need to be emptied of self and filled with the Holy Spirit. The only way to do that is to surrender ourselves to the Lord for healing and consecration. This process of committing ourselves to the Lord is vital. We want to have a heart that says, *"Whatever it looks like, I choose You. I will go where You say to go. I will be who You called me to be. Just say the word."* Just as Moses wouldn't go without God's presence in Exodus 33:15, we must also have hearts so unified with God that His words are ours. If you feel resistance in this area and don't feel fully surrendered yet it is okay! This is a continual process. The Lord takes us deeper and deeper as we mature. As we ask for help, the Lord is gracious to help us surrender each area in obedience.

Hiddenness is one way the Lord uses to equip us and draw us closer to His heart so we can be trusted with everything He wants to pour out. The Lord often uses our hidden seasons to work on those vulnerable places. It is a time to be real with ourselves and God in seeking deep healing and deliverance. In His kindness, He leads us to repentance and reveals those areas we tend to hide from ourselves. Even those trained in healing and deliverance need refreshing and continued healing. As Paul said in Philippians 3:12, none of us have arrived, yet we press on to be more like Christ and to have our capacity expanded as vessels of His Glory.

In John 15:1-2, Jesus speaks about this continual process of becoming like Him and the consecration required to continue producing more fruit. He says, "I am the true Grapevine, and my Father is the Gardener. He cuts off every branch of mine that doesn't produce fruit, and He prunes the branches that do bear fruit so they will produce even more" (NLT). Later He directs us twice to remain in Him and Him in us as this is the only way to produce much fruit and to please the Father. Apart from Him, we can produce nothing and that which is not in Him is thrown into the fire. We want to build what will last intergenerationally. We want to build on the solid rock of God's Word rather than building in our flesh on shifting sand (Matthew 7:24-27). Following Jesus as He leads us on a continual journey of healing and consecration will ensure we build on solid rock that lasts. It also ensures that we can stand and sustain the more that He desires to give and produce much fruit.

It's important to note that sometimes the Holy Spirit leads us through pruning for an upgrade. We may have taken necessary steps for healing, deliverance, and continued consecration, yet the Lord will call us to a deeper level of surrender, maturity, and renewed thinking to expand our capacity for oneness with Christ. This allows Him to release a greater level of Glory within and around us.

Inner Healing Activation:

Psychology shows the healing power of healthy relationships when it comes to recovering from trauma and thriving in life. We heal best while in a community because we were created for togetherness! We often need ministers to accelerate healing and deliverance in areas we tend to hide from ourselves. There is power in agreement to bring freedom. We need both deep meaningful fellowship with God and those He leads us to as we walk out our call.

A great way to receive inner healing and connect to the voice of God is through Immanuel journaling & Lectio Divina (listening prayer). A quick exercise for this is to turn on some instrumental worship music or worship until you feel God's Presence. Write out a

Stewardship

few things you are thankful for or appreciate about God or His creation. According to Dr. Karl D. Lehman, the creator of the Immanuel Method, thankfulness is scientifically proven to create a positive connection pathway in our brains with God and with others. Next, write out your concerns and listen for God's response. It can help to read scripture to hear the Lord speak.

You can also use listening prayer to plan with God. Review and surrender your calendar to Him. Invite Him into your planning. Ask Him what's on His heart and what He wants you to know for the day as well as for each planning period.

We can practice His presence throughout the day by simply taking time to remind ourselves God is always present with us, especially in our time of need (Psalm 46:1). Ask throughout the day, *"God what do you think of this? What's on your heart right now? What would you like me to know? Is there anything you want someone around me to know right now?"* Psalms 100:4-5 says our thanksgiving and praise opens the gates of Heaven. Thank Him often because He is good!

Inner Healing & Deliverance

There are many incredible ministries for inner healing and deliverance. Please pray and invite the Lord into your healing journey. He will highlight who you can trust in learning the process as well as the right timing.

ABOUT THE AUTHOR

Lenora is the founder of Championing Champions. She has a background in counseling, inner healing, and career coaching. After years of studying design as a passion, the Lord called her into branding for Kingdom Entrepreneurs. She has a passion for prophetically seeking God's heart with clients and applying what is revealed to the design process. She has a vision of partnering with the Holy Spirit in branding an army of Kingdom entrepreneurs — readying them for their unveiling and advancement as Kingdom Influencers. Her unique skill set cultivates an atmosphere of encounter-based branding, high-quality design, and breakthroughs to elevate clients to their next level. Lenora has several years of training in the prophetic and offers prophetic business consultations where she cultivates time for encounters providing direction in business and personal breakthroughs. She thrives in equipping and empowering Kingdom entrepreneurs with creative vision and equipping them to walk out the fullness of their call. Lenora is also the founder of The Hope Broadcast, a shop with products to make Jesus famous, and Raising Up Revivalists, a community and blog for revivalist moms.

TO CONNECT WITH LENORA:

Email: championingchampions@gmail.com
Website: http://www.championingthechampions.com/
Facebook: Facebook @ChampioningTheChampions
Instagram: @championingthechampions
Book A Call: Calendly.com/championingthechampions

CHAPTER 6

God's Truth Through Simplicity

Valery B. Ireland, USA
TRANSFORMATIONAL HEALTH COACH

THE JOURNEY OF BECOMING

Embarking on a transformative journey demands acknowledging the depth of our struggles and finding the courage to pursue change. In my own life, I was burdened by unresolved heart wounds from neglect and abuse. Seeking validation, approval, and acceptance jeopardized my well-being. For years, I sought comfort in food, trying to numb the pain temporarily. However, the void of inadequacy grew insatiable, and my obsession with food and endless diets to control my weight spiraled out of control, leaving me defeated and disgusted. I found myself trapped in a vicious cycle of feeding guilt and shame within the confines of a food jail.

In 1999, at my lowest point, I had to break free from the painful emotional cycle profoundly impacting my health with major depression, disease, isolation, and disillusionment of my existence. The moment arrived when my life flashed before me, prompting a decision to seek help. Hungry for change, I welcomed support and surrendered control. It was then that I encountered the all-loving, all-knowing, all-powerful, all-forgiving God, who was not the punitive one I was led to believe in. A tremendous relief washed over me, knowing I was no longer alone in this battle.

Thus began my journey into the unknown. Climbing towards health and healing, I carried a heavy load. Through a complex process of rigid plans, I questioned labels and untangled misconceptions and confusion, while healing, dealing, forgiving, letting go, and letting God be God journey, paying a high price for my transformation.

In the early stages of my healing journey, a revelation hit me- a deep desire to give back. Although I didn't fully grasp its significance at first, God guided me through each step, leading me to opportunities for growth. My path unfolded through continuous education, diverse job experiences, and witnessing soul-stirring transformations. In pursuit of simplicity and truth, I dismantled overcomplicated systems and peeled back layers to uncover the core truths of existence and my own identity. This era expanded my relationship with God, leading to a profound transformation of the soul. As I embraced Kingdom entrepreneurship and in response to God's calling, my business Empowered to the Core was birthed.

Rooted in my personal and professional experiences, this business emerged as a transformative process through self-discovery and strategies to pave the way for self-mastery, and the liberation from the shackles of food, weight, and diets. Emphasizing health and healing first, the process is sustainable, and the weight release is a natural byproduct. To become *empowered at the core* level is indispensable to first become aware of what is disempowering through beliefs, traditions, and lies.

In my journey of self-discovery and transformation, I've come to understand that it's not just about what we eat or how we eat that matters, but also why we eat and what eats at us internally. We become what we consume, as our bodies interpret food as information, and each nutrient serves a specific purpose. However, in our fast-paced lives, we are often disconnected from the food we consume. Additionally, societal conditioning leads us to believe certain emotions are not meant to be expressed, and we turn to specific foods to suppress them. This not only keeps us trapped in a cycle of emotional eating but also results in unexpressed emotions becoming stored within our cells, creating physical blocks and unwanted weight. It's essential to recognize the intimate connection between our emotional well-being and our relationship with food in order to achieve optimal health and function.

It's time to expose the sources contributing to the widespread struggles that prevail in our world today. Despite the abundance of information available, many still find themselves trapped in cycles of unnecessary suffering. The health system is at the tipping point of disaster. Overconsumption of food, stress-induced eating, unresolved trauma, toxin overload, and a relentless pursuit of convenience have taken a toll on our health. When we eat convenience over necessity our bodies suffer, leading to weight gain, sickness, and disease. These health challenges persist as we remain disconnected from the reality of our true nature, and the steep decline is from the choices we make, which clash with the inherent design of our bodies to function optimally. The perplexity deepens as we ponder how a multi-billion-dollar industry can leave the majority sick and suffering. Among this chaos, the food industry, thriving on lies and deception, has evolved into a realm of increasing corruption. Power-hungry individuals design systems grounded in deception, cynically laughing at the expense of our health and finances, while poisoning the vital fuel we consume. Corporations exploit people, prioritizing profit over well-being, skillfully manipulating us with marketing tactics, addictive ingredients, and unethical practices contributing to a cycle of dependency and illness. Similarly, the weight-loss industry perpetuates conflicting narratives steering us towards the false ideology claiming the way to health is by going on a diet. Everyone is pushing the diet agenda, leading us from one imprisoning perspective to another, counting calories, and even eliminating whole food groups. Countless programs, pills, and potions promise quick fixes, but they often overlook the true needs of individuals which complicates the quest for well-being. Cultural norms and traditions further perpetuate this cycle. Mainstream media brainwash us and social media bombard us to believe unrealistic standards exerting immense pressure, perpetuating false beliefs about appearance and eating habits, and fostering fear-based decision-making.

Reflecting on the biblical metaphor, "As the serpent deceived Eve, so minds may be corrupted from the simplicity in Christ" (2 Corinthians 11:3, NKJV).

God's Truth Through Simplicity

We recognize the importance of discarding societal expectations and seek wisdom in choosing well, rooted in the truth. This journey encompasses healing both the body and soul, detoxifying from physical toxins and emotional burdens stored within. It's time to break free from these destructive patterns and reclaim our health and well-being. By uncovering the truth behind these industries and embracing a wholeness approach to health, we can break free from the grip of deception and live authentically empowered lives.

Throughout history, food has been elevated to an idolized status. We use it to celebrate, mourn, entertain, fuel, love, show hospitality, and care for people in tangible ways, and also for comfort. The truth is, we find ourselves in a culture of gluttony, where overeating is encouraged and even celebrated as a solution to cope with life's challenges. Messages like, *"A pint of ice cream will help heal your broken heart"* and *"You deserve pizza and wine after a hard day,"* contribute to the habit of turning to food to fix problems instead of seeking divine intervention for God to address.

I urge you not to underestimate the profound influence wielded by food considering its pivotal role in the fall of man. Reflect on how humanity, represented by Adam and Eve, lost dominion over the Earth—through food! And the temptation did not end there! Even Jesus in the desert faced food temptation, but He, fully aware of His identity, resisted by speaking the word of truth. This is not a trivial matter! For as long as the adversary manipulates food, constantly pushing us toward disease, exploiting the underestimated temptation of food, and fostering gluttony, we play directly into the enemy's strategy to cunningly exploit this vulnerability, seeking to divide and conquer, doing everything possible to separate people from God. We must remain vigilant.

As stated in John 10:10, "The thief does not come except to steal, and to kill, and to destroy. I have come that they may have life and that they may have it more abundantly" (NKJV). There's a fierce spiritual battle at play, with the enemy seeking to steal health, kill body function, and destroy body image. Recognizing the significance of this struggle is essential. The temptation of food is a potent force, intertwined with the spiritual realm, where our choices become pivotal in the ongoing spiritual warfare. Understanding the historical parallels, from the fall of man to the testing of Jesus, sheds light on the intricate role food plays in the spiritual and physical realms. It prompts a call to heightened awareness and discernment in our journey toward health and well-being.

When our Heavenly Father crafted the world, everything was good—every bit of it. Man and woman were created in His image, in a state of complete physical perfection: cells, tissues, and organs functioned in perfect harmony. Food and herbs in their natural state, served to heal, fuel, and bring joy. Healthy is our natural state, and natural is simple. What's unnatural and complex are the junk foods loaded with additives, preservatives, and artificial flavors and colors. When our Heavenly Father created the world, everything was good, including the food provided for nourishment. However, in today's world, food has been corrupted with additives, preservatives, and artificial ingredients. Yet, it remains a gift from God, intended to nourish and restore us to His original design.

In a world filled with manipulation and deception, we crave truth. Truth without blame or shame. We've been fed enough lies and led like sheep to the slaughter. I've experienced this darkness firsthand and have been set free. It's time to reject the lies that lead us astray and embrace the simplicity of God's provision. Only then can we break free from the cycle of deception and experience true liberation. I've experienced this darkness firsthand

and have been set free. I have been pruned, primed, and positioned to recognize what's out of order and out of alignment with God. Like me, others need to break free from these chains.

Despite the pain and struggle I faced God had me endure and conquer which now fuels my purpose. The very thing that tried to take me out, God is using for good, and now I stand with the authority He graciously bestowed upon me. As we see in Genesis 5:20, "But as for you, you meant evil against me; but God meant it for good, in order to bring it about as it is this day, to save many people alive" (NKJV). God, the ultimate recycler, ingeniously uses every lived experience.

"And we know that all things work together for good to those who love God, to those who are the called according to His purpose." - Romans 8:28, NKJV

God has my story and my *yes* in His hands, to empower those who would not fight for themselves. I have been blessed to be a blessing, and my impact goes as deep and wide as I'm willing to do the inner work. Being healed and healthy makes me more useful to God.

As an ambassador for the Kingdom, I am entrusted with implementing God's principles of health and wellness. Through Heaven's Health Program, I aim to dispel complexity, expose lies, and uproot corruption within the realm of health. My mission is to realign individuals with God's original intent, restoring their health, reclaiming their body function and image, and renewing their relationship with food.

At the core of this journey lies the principle of simplicity. Health, I've come to realize, is not complicated; it is our inherent nature. As we embrace this simplicity and align ourselves with God's design, we can experience true healing and restoration.

As spiritual beings inhabiting physical bodies with souls comprising the mind, will, and emotions, we are called to tend to all aspects of our being. This involves viewing life through the lens of truth, embracing simplicity, and shedding emotional baggage that clouds our judgment. While our emotions are valid expressions of our humanity, they should not dictate our actions. Instead, we must learn to work with and through our emotions, emerging stronger and more resilient in the process.

True healing and health can only be attained by following a simple path—one that prioritizes nourishing both body and soul. Through my calling, I endeavor to extend this breakthrough to others, guiding them through the process of learning new concepts, identifying limiting beliefs, and implementing methods for compounding results. Together, we discover that food is a gift from God, meant to fuel, nourish, and heal our bodies, rather than serving as a mere emotional crutch.

I offer the keys to unlocking the core essence of one's being, empowering individuals to embrace their true identity and fulfill their God-given purpose. Sustainability requires a holistic approach, addressing not only the physical but also the emotional aspects of our well-being. This entails delving into deeply rooted emotions that may be hindering our progress—a process that is both possible and necessary for true transformation. By facing these emotions head-on, we open the door for God's healing and restoration in our lives.

Empowered to the Core is a business of transformation that breaks off the lies and complexity surrounding health, demonstrating God's truth through simplicity. At its core, the program aims to empower individuals to reclaim control over their lives and embrace self-mastery and freedom.

The program begins by diving into the fundamental ABCs: Awareness, Behavior, and Change. Through deepening awareness, participants uncover the underlying reasons behind their behaviors and cultivate a hunger for meaningful change. Education plays a pivotal role, providing insights into health enemies, food biology, and the psychology of eating. Armed with this knowledge, participants make informed choices aligned with God's original design for their well-being.

Mentorship, rooted in personal experience and faith, provides guidance, accountability, and support throughout the journey. The MONA method, inspired by a Monarch butterfly, serves as a transformative approach, guiding individuals to tap into their inner power and overcome emotional barriers. Emotion Regulation Strategies are also integrated, empowering individuals to embrace their journey fully.

As participants progress, they experience tangible results and embody the MONA Effect – a state of liberation from food bondage, fully activated to live according to God's original intent. Ultimately, Empowered to the Core isn't just about shedding pounds or achieving a certain body image; it's about reclaiming inherent health, vitality, and wholeness. Through simplicity, truth, and alignment with God's intention, individuals thrive in body, mind, and spirit, becoming the best version of themselves – empowered, confident, and free.

Adherence to Kingdom principles sets us apart, empowering us to drive positive change and expand the Kingdom. By integrating these principles into our lives and businesses, we become catalysts for transformation. God seeks individuals who are skilled, competent, and capable. The question remains: *How will you choose to show up?*

In the Kingdom of God, simplicity reigns supreme. Simplicity is not just a principle to live by; it's a journey toward a life and business that resonates with our essence. The essence of truth is revealed when expressed simply, transcending unnecessary complexities. In simplicity, we find efficiency, effectiveness, and a more direct route to our objectives. God's wisdom illuminates straightforward paths, guiding us with clarity and purpose. As we embrace this simplicity in our lives and businesses, we unlock the full potential of God's guidance, leading to success and fulfillment.

"For our boasting is this: the testimony of our conscience that we conducted ourselves in the world in simplicity and godly sincerity, not with fleshly wisdom but by the grace of God, and more abundantly toward you" -2 Corinthians 1:12, NKJV

As Kingdom entrepreneurs, our mission is clear: to solve problems and serve God's people according to His will. Drawing from our own breakthroughs, we infuse our work with empathy, compassion, and kindness, magnifying our impact. The key to our success lies in embracing the principle of simplicity, rooted in truth. Truth, inherently simple yet powerful, disrupts falsehoods and calls us to higher standards. By aligning ourselves with God and boldly standing in truth, we expose corruption and prioritize the well-being of His people. In partnering with truth, we align ourselves with Jesus, who embodies truth itself.

Imagine a life free from excess possessions, commitments, and distractions, navigating with ease and purpose. Simplicity teaches the art of value, free from fear and false identity, where sharing generously comes naturally. It's about shedding layers of pretense, freeing us from cages of our own making because the world of pretend is a cage, not a cozy cocoon.

The dance between truth and simplicity becomes apparent in the ABCs of Awareness, Behavior, and Change. By fostering awareness, understanding behaviors, and embracing change, transformation unfolds organically.

Peeling back the layers to find our core essence is a beautiful process, it connects us with our true identity. Making the complicated simple requires effort and creativity; it's an art. The MONA method, inspired by the simplicity of a Monarch butterfly, leads to transformation from within. Distilling concepts into manageable steps facilitates understanding and prompts action.

In a world that glorifies complexity, true power resides in simplicity. Through simplicity, the noise is quieted, preparing us for spiritual connection. Imagine entering God's presence with empty hands and a pure heart, ready to give and receive authentically. As we commit to simplicity rooted in truth, our lives and businesses thrive, reflecting the brilliance of God's guiding light.

Lastly, perhaps you have heard of the **K.I.S.S.** approach. There are many meanings, some are nicer and more impactful: **K**eep **I**t **S**imple **S**illy, or **S**weetheart. It's a clever reminder that we get to **K**eep **I**t **S**o **S**imple. It leads to a fulfilling, sustainable journey in the Kingdom of God because the **K**ingdom **I**s **S**uper **S**imple!

So, my friend, carry these thoughts with you, letting simplicity guide you toward a more profound, intentional way of living and working in your business. Align with God's command for clarity, focus, and do-ability. Let simplicity be your compass in navigating the complexities of life and business, particularly in the pillar of health and the way you relate to food. I invite you to join me on this journey of empowerment, in pursuit of truth, fostering a discerning approach to knowledge with a commitment to authenticity. Together let's dismantle the lies, embrace simplicity, and unlock the core essence of our being. And remember to implement my master key: Look through the transparent lens of truth, and flow with the pureness of simplicity.

ABOUT THE AUTHOR

Valery B Ireland, a seasoned Transformational Health Coach brings over a decade of experience in health and nutrition training, coupled with a deep commitment to healing and fortifying the body through movement-based modalities. Her passion lies in empowering women to triumph over defeat, frustration, and powerlessness in their relationship with food, fostering lasting transformation.

Dedicated to her roles as a loving wife and devoted mother of two brilliant boys, Valery also cherishes moments of family joy with their beloved dog. Beyond her mission to liberate women from the chains of food-related powerlessness, she thrives in the role of a baseball mom, supporting her husband, a Doctor of Osteopathic Medicine. Nature walks and creative artistic expressions are her sources of joy and rejuvenation.

Through her journey from personal struggles to an agent of positive change, Valery, born and raised in Peru, exemplifies resilience and compassion. With a Bachelor of Science in Applied Behavior Psychology and more than 15 years in the field, she endeavors to guide women toward holistic health, encouraging transformative and sustainable change.

TO CONNECT WITH VALERY:

Email: valery@empoweredtothecore.com
Facebook: facebook.com/valery.ireland
Instagram: instagram.com/valerybireland
LinkedIn: http://linkedin.com/in/valery-b-ireland-4670349/
Website: https://www.empoweredtothecore.com
Book A Call: https://bit.ly/DiscoveryCallWithVal

CHAPTER 7

Truth and Rest

Janet Taylor, USA
SOLUTIONIST - DIGITAL & VIRTUAL BUSINESSES

Take My yoke upon you and learn from Me, for I am gentle and lowly in heart, and you will find rest for your souls.
-Matthew 11:29, NKJV

I HAVE BEEN DECEIVED, IN BOTH LIFE AND THE CHURCH

In 1998, at the age of thirty-four, I had already had a lifetime of misogyny and patriarchy. Being the youngest daughter of a military man and later navigating the corporate world as a strong woman, I witnessed that damaging attitude all my life. Naturally, I didn't question it when I found it in the church on steroids after accepting Christ for salvation.

Truth and Rest

For ten years, I worked hard to be a "good Christian:" teaching Bible studies, leading prayer groups, and homeschooling. I did all the things I believed I was supposed to do as a "submissive wife." Life, however, began to unravel. My husband and I were always arguing; not only about unresolved issues from before we began attending church but also about the Bible itself. My oldest child, who was fifteen at the time, was fighting for independence from being under what I now understand was a legalistic upbringing. My youngest child, ten years old, had recently endured surgeries on her feet that limited her mobility and impacted other areas of her health. Consequently, she found solace and safety by retreating in silence from all the noise of the house. My health was being impacted by the sudden onset of asthma and autoimmune issues which took center stage. Advice from the church and Christian friends was *less than helpful* at the time. This is when I started my journey to *becoming truly liberated* and recognized I had been deceived.

Life was happening as it had never happened before. Amid stress, bitterness, and tears, I knew this was not what I was reading as promised in the Bible. I am reading promises of rest from weariness, peace for anxiety, and the desires of my heart. *What was I missing?* It turns out, I was missing everything.

BETRAYED. CONNED. DUPED. VICTIMIZED.

The most damaging part of deception is you do not know that it is happening. I believed everything other people told me, including when I started to attend church in 1997. As the third daughter of a career military man from Texas, etiquette and proper manners were required. *"Yes ma'am", "yes sir",* and *"please and thank you"* is the norm, and you would be reminded if you did not comply. As adults, my sisters and I still lined up in age order when my dad called us to a room. It is ingrained. Growing up in Texas, deep in the Bible Belt, reinforced my need to submit to others with little thought of myself. It is part of the culture to put others first, always smile, and speak in friendly tones, especially to strangers. Southern hospitality is not just for the movies. In the 70's and 80's, when feminism was well established, traditional male and female roles were still expected in my home. When my mother worked outside the home, she was still the homemaker. In a state where corporal punishment is still legal, children were seen and not heard, so I did not question authority much. I realized I believed everything anyone said because I perceived everyone as more important than me without question. Seeing myself as "less than" or "not enough" is most definitely a conditioned trauma response.

Then you will call upon Me and go and pray to Me, and I will listen to you. And you will seek Me and find Me, when you search for Me with all your heart. - Jeremiah 29:12-13, NKJV

As I began to pray and read the Bible for myself, I started to see scriptures that I would call "outliers" from an academic perspective. Something was obviously missing in my understanding. I asked God to show me who I was and what I was created to be. I began to discern the scriptures that clearly illustrated the intention and oneness of the Creator. I have now come to accept that I am wholly God's daughter and all that comes as a child of the Most High God. I was created for a purpose and that is the same purpose as a male was created. The writer of Genesis uses words that are both genderless and plural when referring to God. Even when translated into English, Genesis 1:26 uses plural language. "Then God said, "Let Us make man in Our image, according to Our likeness" (NKJV). This was freeing for me to understand God has no gender. God is not like my earthly father, who often was controlling and manipulative. Having difficulty calling God "father," I began to refer to the Godhead - Father, Son, and Holy Spirit - as Them because of this verse. As I continue to unlearn and relearn about my place in the Kingdom, I realize God is not angry nor condemning as I had been led to believe. This is an ongoing revelation of God's spiritual fruit as I walk through life (Gal. 5:22).

My identity as an image bearer, now filled with the same Holy Spirit who was present during creation, who raised Jesus from the dead, and the same Spirit Jesus promised to send, changed my entire perspective on my life and future. I was shocked to know how many people already knew about this freedom; just walking around, living their lives in victory and abundance, enjoying the rest, peace, and the desires of their hearts. First, I was mad! *"Why didn't I know? Why didn't someone tell me?"*

God gently answered, *"They don't know there are people, like you, who have been and are still being deceived. It is their own deception. They do not understand how many people in the world are in bondage. So, I want you to go and tell your story."*

My focus is clear: amplify women's voices who have a message to help heal humanity. For too long, the woman's voice has been silenced in the world, especially in the church. My heart's desire is to help them wherever they are in their journey. This inspired the creation of a social enterprise: On Purpose, For Purpose, With Purpose Enterprises LLC. Its goal: provide opportunities for women with powerful messages of overcoming struggles to break down roadblocks and barriers that keep them from their personal journey to becoming truly liberated, secure in their identity, and living with peace by resting in God's love.

In Ephesians 2:10, we are told that we are His workmanship, created in Christ Jesus for good works, which God prepared beforehand that we should walk in them. *Isn't that incredible?* Our purpose in creation is for the good of humanity. We have always been in Christ, even before the creation of our Earth, and Adam and Eve stopped believing God because of the words of another. That one simple understanding of identity could change what someone believes about themselves and give them direction for their life: created on purpose, for purpose, and given the opportunity to live with purpose.

I have always been entrepreneurial. As a child, I was constantly looking for ways to make money. As a teenager, I begged my mom to sign for me to be an Avon representative. Over the years, I have sold with different MLM (multi-level marketing) companies. It seemed easy and inexpensive to get started but I didn't know how to market and sell. I sold products to friends and family and generally became a nuisance to everyone. I was always focused on the sales and profits but never on the person I was begging for the sale. My sister and I started our first actual business together when I was nineteen. We bought and sold jewelry. It was fun but we spent more than we sold. Again, I had the wrong focus, but the dream remained.

After leaving the corporate world in 1997 to stay home with my only child at the time, I offered my human resources and administrative skills to people who I already knew. I did make money and I was able to work around my schedule. Soon, my schedule included putting my child back in daycare 2-3 days a week. The exact opposite of why I left my good-paying corporate job. I continued to see my business as a means to an end (money), not about focusing on helping the person I was working with, and certainly not the goal for me to be a stay-at-home mother to my 3-year-old. Ironically, I have always been a stickler for good customer service when it came to serving me. Me. Me. Me. Talk about missing the mark.

Now I am in a new season of life, with grown children leading their own lives, while still caring for my Mom different times throughout the year. I began to ask God about opportunities for making money without being bound to a corporate office. Doors began to open that brought me in contact with different people who were talking about being an entrepreneur driven by being Kingdom-minded. This was much different from being a Christian in business. This focuses on seeking first what could be done for the Kingdom of God and the people touched by our products and services. When we do that, all else will be added as Matthew 6:33 tells us. I began to see more opportunities to live from the peace and rest of my Provider.

In 2016, I started a Facebook page to document my journey to repurpose my life. Eventually, it was renamed *Becoming Truly Liberated*. This was the first business I was focused on helping other people and not just on making a profit. Its mission: To guide women in understanding why their lives, stories, and voices are vital for such a time as this. It was my introduction to starting a business for reasons beyond the obvious. Like other Kingdom businesses, my focus shifted to being dedicated to stewarding my gifts and serving each other in a mutually beneficial relationship.

And He Himself gave some to be apostles, some prophets, some evangelists, and some pastors and teachers, for the equipping of the saints for the work of ministry, for the edifying of the Body of Christ, till we all come to the unity of the faith and of the knowledge of the Son of God - Ephesians 4:11-16, NKJV.

Our collective message and gifts are needed as part of the tapestry of the Kingdom. Loving the Body of Christ and helping her grow and thrive is all I am focused on in my life and business. Until the Body of Christ shines brighter than anything else in the world, she will not have the impact that she is intended to have. We must begin the process of combatting the deceptions and lies of the "religion of Christianity" and replacing it with Truth. This begins with raising the awareness within the church that there is more to what we are being taught. Learning to question and examine scriptures with a Kingdom lens, while strengthening, encouraging, and comforting those who struggle in their bondage. We will not be able to shift the ways of the world until we are healed, whole, and standing out as different from those who do not have Christ. Statistically, there is no difference between professing Christians when it comes to divorce, poverty, illness, substance abuse, and division as in the unbelieving world. *"What do we have to offer humanity if we are not any different?"* This is not what God intended for us. He came to Earth as Emmanuel-God with us. He died on the cross to pay the penalty of death so we could have life abundantly. Now we need to learn how to do that in every area of living including how we make money and live out each day in service to humanity. Only when Kingdom people offer solutions to the problems of the world will the world become what God intended when it was first created. Shae Bynes, Founder of Kingdom Driven Entrepreneurs, declared on Day 1 of Firestarter School, *"Once you step your feet into the water of being a Kingdom Driven Entrepreneur, you will not be able to imagine doing business without partnering with the presence of our awesome and limitless God* (Bynes)."

Knowing that I am a co-heir and ambassador of the Kingdom of God with all the privileges it brings transformed my approach to life and also my business. Living from the overflow of Holy Spirit, aligned with the fruits of the Spirit in every area of business (products and services), allows me to shift my perspective from toil and fretting to rest and releasing. The core values of love, joy, peace, patience, kindness, goodness, faithfulness, gentleness, and self-control found in Galatians 5:22 combined with what we learn about love in 1 Corinthians 13 is the basis for all my decisions in business. This focus on unity allows me to make decisions without anxiety about the outcome while embracing oneness helps me to learn to love like He loves us.

Learning to hear from God and discerning His guidance takes time and practice. I have been seeking wisdom and understanding for over ten years now and have just scratched the surface of what I know God has for me. We can only hear as much as we understand and believe, so we might get things wrong sometimes, but thankfully God is so much bigger. He sees our hearts and our intent and meets us where we are with grace and patience. We can apply this same attitude to our clients and customers as we learn to stay in step with the Spirit and continue to rest in our identity.

In the early 90's, I was part of an organization called The Junior Chamber of Commerce (Jaycees). Their creed still comes to mind often as I think about life. It says, "We believe that faith in God gives meaning and purpose to human life; that the brotherhood of man transcends the sovereignty of nations; that economic justice can best be won by free men through free enterprise; that government should be of laws rather than of men; that earth's great treasure lies in human personality and that service to humanity is the best work of life." That sounds like a Kingdom perspective to me.

While the rest of the world focuses on surviving, manipulating, and making profits without regard to people, my business, *With Purpose*, is focused on thriving, people, abiding, and stewardship. It's all about Them (Trinity) and them (people). Kingdom is win/win and give/give. There is no competition, only collaboration with love being the center of it all. Pedro Adao, Founder of 100X, wrote the following in his Field of Favor workbook, "We prove our love for our clients by making offers of help that bring breakthrough" (Adao).

When we recognize and acknowledge the bigger picture of our role as a Kingdom Entrepreneur, our influence and impact as the Body of Christ will skyrocket. When we are genuinely focused on the person and not on the product or service we want them to buy, we will prosper while they prosper. We do not have to manipulate anyone to buy our products or services because we only care about what they need.

Sowing and reaping from my place of rest is how God gave me my unconventional approach to providing services to help other Kingdom businesses. By offering *Name Your Price* packages for tech and administrative solutions, I can create income while fostering an atmosphere of low-pressure friendship and understanding for women who are overwhelmed with learning completely new skills to enter the marketplace. I have taken courses to increase my knowledge and skills in the areas of technology and digital marketing where I learned how to calculate my rates and fees. People may not understand and even criticize me for this decision, but learning to listen and abide in His heart and accepting my new creation identity is the key to this type of life. I no longer believe I am "less than" someone else and their opinion of my decisions. This is not the first time God has impressed upon me to step out in faith. It gets easier every time. Jesus said don't be anxious about your life, don't worry about the essentials of living. So, I won't.

"Look at the birds of the air, for they neither sow nor reap nor gather into barns; yet your heavenly Father feeds them. Are you not of more value than they?" - Matthew 6:26, NKJV

Becoming aware of what I believe and why I believe it has been the most freeing exercise I have ever encountered. It has also been the most difficult. It takes courage to be introspective. Whether you are eighteen or eighty-one, understanding fully where your beliefs come from and the way they impact both you and the world around you changes everything. To investigate what formed the beliefs you hold takes time, but it is beyond words to describe the freedom and peace it gives you when you can begin to make life decisions based on your own personal statement of beliefs. Every area of your life is touched by this personal set of beliefs from relationships to business to health. I invite you to begin your own exploration. I will be here to encourage, support, and guide you in taking the first step to go deeper in your journey.

FROM AWARENESS TO ACCELERATION
TWELVE ACTIVATIONS FOR YOUR KINGDOM HEART AND MIND

AWARENESS of misaligned beliefs causes you to ASK for revelation wisdom. *Who or what have you been agreeing with or to?* Your agreement what opens your heart and mind to whatever is influencing you.

AGREE and ALIGN with what God shows you. Research and reconcile what you believed, why you believed it, and if anything needs to be relearned.

AFFIRM and ABIDE by regularly declaring what you have come to know as Truth. Some things in life may be *facts*, such as your circumstances but declarations are reminders of what God has shown you to be *true* in His word and His love for you; not positive words to convince yourself something that is fact is not. Focusing on what may be missing from your understanding of the Truth in your circumstances will allow you to abide in Him.

As an AMBASSADORS with AUTHORITY from Christ, you can become the most loving and encouraging person in the room, releasing victorious language to strengthen, encourage, or comfort every person and situation you encounter.

Being ALIVE with ABUNDANCE is a gift from Jesus. Join something bigger than you could possibly do on your own. Work in collaboration with others for ACCOUNTABILITY and ACCELERATION. The only reason there is any darkness in the world is because the light has not shown up there yet. Who and how you are influencing the people who are watching you is important to you and them.

No matter where you are in your journey of Kingdom living, I want to encourage you not to skip steps. If God elevates you then Go! But don't skip steps in the process. If you work in your own strength, you will not be ready to handle what is coming. You can prepare. You can work to get in a position to receive. When you are ready, it will be easy, and it will flow. Forcing anything in life could cause ripples that take years to straighten out. Trust the process and always give honor to those who have influenced and taught you.

ABOUT THE AUTHOR

Janet is a lifelong dreamer, visionary and entrepreneur currently navigating country life on family land in Texas. Family is everything to her and she currently shares custody of her mom, the beloved Nana (a.k.a. Lee) with her sisters, Shari and Donna. She loves being Mom to the most amazing adults, B & R, as well as Nanny to the dynamic duo. After living with all four generations in one house during the pandemic, she misses the chaos and craziness of a full house but treasures the possibilities of what is to come as she rediscovers and redefines life after sixty with her passions for purpose and people in the Kingdom of God!

TO CONNECT WITH JANET:

Email: yourfriends@becomingtrulyliberated.com
Website: https://www.becomingtrulyliberated.com
Facebook: @BecomingTrulyLiberated
              @DigitalAndVirtualBusinessSolutions

OTHER BOOKS:

- *Becoming Truly Liberated in a World of Lies by the Patriarchy* (In Revision)
- *Journals and Trackers:* Reflection: Quiet Time Meditation Journal for Calming Your Mind and Finding Peace; The Way of Love: Learning to Love One Another Prayer; Affirmation and Reflection Journal - 100 Days of Love; My Daily Tracker & Wellness Log: A 52 Week Daily Tracker & Wellness Log: Reminders in Large Print for Seniors and the Easily Distracted
- *Digital Coloring Book Collections - Monthly Themes*

CHAPTER 8

Integrity - Who's Going to Know?

Elizabeth Kirsten, UK
SELF-DISCOVERY COACH

"And as for me, thou upholdest me in mine integrity, and settest me before thy face forever." - Psalms 41:12, KJV

Honesty and integrity are two Kingdom principles not found in the marketplace today. Proverbs 11:3 states, "The integrity of the upright guides them but the crookedness of the treacherous destroys them" (KJV). Powerful words! Integrity guides while treachery destroys. Though we can't always see how *the crookedness of the treacherous destroys them* regarding regular business practice, we'd be short-sighted to disregard biblical principles that will ultimately prosper us and not harm us. We must not

Integrity - Who's Going to Know?

lose sight of our compass, Jesus. Most civilizations operate according to biblical principles and morals which underpin their legal system. Rather than focus on convenient loopholes for the few or making a fast buck, it would serve a higher purpose to gain wisdom regarding legislation! I believe these two important Kingdom principles are the firm foundation of any business venture because they are part of our Saviour: The Way, THE TRUTH, and the Life!

Through applying the word of God to promote my business, indeed designing my business around it, my drive and passion to put a crown on someone else's head, raising them to the fullness of their designed potential facilitate a mutual goal. Revealing treasure, facilitating life skill upgrades, and putting them to use for the benefit of all. In so doing, I honour God by fulfilling my calling, and loving others as I love myself. God took me from a crazy unfulfilled life, lifted me up, and put a crown on my head. I had failed to recognize my true identity in Him and His rich love for me. This fundamental, no, foundational truth had bypassed me. I behaved as an orphan, and orphans don't recognize a crown. Until I learned my Father valued me, I was hardly able to adequately convey this truth to others. Reading and quoting the truth is vastly different from application. A business that recognizes the value of others through their self-improvement, whilst achieving personal and corporate goals. A platform where you aren't competing against others, but rather wanting others to succeed. I want you to do better than me, to be more successful!

Honesty with strong moral principles leads to integrity. The word *honesty* has a root which means to be honourable and respected. In definitions from Oxford Languages, and I quote *integrity* is late middle English from the Latin *integritas* and French *integrite*. It means a state of being whole or complete. Referring to a person, it points to the concept of living by one's values and principles. Further, the definition for *completeness* is quoted as, "A framework comprising beliefs, moral principles, ethics, and standards."

These two principles go hand in glove for me. My forty years of experience in the corporate and retail world left me feeling these two essential aspects of humanity are usually absent or at best, lacking throughout leadership and management, which trickles down to frontline services.

I wasn't always a person of honesty or integrity. As a young woman, I had risen very quickly to a managerial position in retail fashion, managing a store sixty miles from home. In our store, we had a franchise (another company) with a section in our

Integrity - Who's Going to Know?

shop. It was Christmas and we were all going out after work to celebrate. We'd all got changed into our gladrags (fine attire), but I had no suitable jewellery. The woman from the franchise said to borrow a necklace from her counter, so against my better judgment, I left bedecked with the snake choker-style neck ornament and locked up the shop for the Christmas break. The following were days off, and when I returned to work I'd forgotten to bring the item back. I assured the franchise manager I'd return it the next day. There was previously an undercurrent of jealousy towards me from the franchise lady. The following day I remembered said item which was now in my purse in my locker. My area manager was in and my train had been delayed making me late; she called me down to the office. Thinking my lateness may be the reason for this, I was shocked when she told me I had been reported for theft of the item. I told her it was in my locker, and that we'd all borrowed stuff. What an excuse! "Borrowing" products which belong to a company is still wrong. I was duly demoted back to sales assistant and returned to my home store. I had learnt a few valuable lessons from that misadventure; financially it had cost me a lot, with a salary reduction, plus the extreme sense of ridicule. It was painful. Fortunately, the manager I worked alongside was kind. With diligence on my part and due recognition on hers, I worked my way back up. I eventually left to become a cash office manager of a large nationwide company. After this and other lessons, I determined honesty was the best policy and to remain true to my morals. I wasn't a follower of Christ, so the teachings and wisdom of the Bible were just faint whispers that harkened from a once-Christian generation. Now thirty-eight years later, I can surely understand the real advantage of being truly integrated with my personal and biblical moral compass. The irony of the choice of a python around my throat, once I became Kingdom-minded, was not lost on me! Honesty didn't always pay off but being misleading for financial or positional superiority and influence has caused great destruction in society. If I can't find a boss, manager, or team leader who applies these important principles, then I'll create an enterprise and become that boss, manager, and team leader. *Why do I want to do this?* To improve people's lives and cheer them on as they prosper! To help others find themselves in a world that shouts, *"You're a nobody"* unless you buy this product or behave a certain way is a valuable commodity. I know where my help comes from Psalm 121:2, "My help comes from the Lord, maker of heaven and earth!" (NIV). To pay that freeing truth forward by introducing people who are in my sphere of influence to their worth is an honour. We are a representative of God Himself, just as Jesus was!

Any business owned by a Kingdom Entrepreneur needs a foundation of integrity, just as a building needs a foundation, cornerstones, structural strength, good electricals, and plumbing, and to cap it, a good roof or ceiling. In the same way, any business needs the integration of these things. It all begins with the blueprint! From writing your vision down to creating documents to work from for conception, birth, and growth, integrity must run through your business, woven in like a tapestry. Your business needs to stand out for all the right reasons. Connecting with your customers should be formed through relational trust, then even when they don't require your service or product any longer, they will advertise it for you!

What I believe to be the underlying foundations of both honour and integrity, Jesus was recorded as declaring to be the greatest commandment, Matthew 22:37-40, to first love God with our heart, mind, and soul, and to also love others as we love ourselves. Personally applied, integrity is all about being true to ourselves and about ourselves, which should be organically incorporated into our business. Our journey and experiences are what influence our character. For this reason, we'd do well to remain aware of how these milestones cause us to act or react on either end of the business spectrum - hectic busyness and a time of crickets! Integrity is recognizing where we've come from and recognizing where our paying customers are in this part of their life journey. We serve the King by serving in His Kingdom.

My business *Life Without Limits* is based around the scripture Matthew 19:26 *"With people this is impossible, but with God all things are possible"* (NIV). This foundational scripture in context is referring to people doing good things to reap the reward of heaven. Jesus' response was there is only one who qualifies! Neither work nor money will make it possible. Yet with God, all things are possible! When we model what we know Jesus did and does, His Kingdom expands, and His people prosper.

Life Without Limits is an umbrella name for a multi-faceted, multi-option coaching and facilitation platform. We partner with individuals to support and encourage *out-of-the-box* thinking by offering solutions with opportunities to connect with other like-minded individuals. It offers a bespoke and unique coaching program to individuals and small groups. Tailor-made to suit personal and group requirements, learning capacity, and desired outcome whilst honing natural skills and learning new ones. The parent company encompasses Wise Women, a subscriber-only group where there are daily nuggets, weekly podcasts, periodic challenges, and online gatherings, aimed at encouraging women of faith and no faith alike. *Proving Proverbs* is a subscriber group for Kingdom people, both men and women, offering like-minded connections whilst introducing and encouraging entrepreneurship. Daisy Chains is a private UK support group for Kingdom women who have experienced marital sexual abuse.

Right now the world needs something or someone to believe in. In a social climate where there is no firm foundation, no set rules, and shifting moral values, we need the truth found in the word of God more than ever. Whilst statements such as "the world is going to hell in a hand cart" subliminally enter into our consciences, my desire is to see people untethered from said handcart, released into basic truths that lead them into asking questions about their own identity, then stepping into the freedom that awaits. If we partner with Kingdom principles and the King himself, we will be working from our salvation - our renewed minds, not working for it!

As I shared earlier, my hope is that my business will stand out by the testimonies of those who have successfully completed modules in the coaching program, through word-of-mouth recommendations and peer reviews on social media platforms. Let my customers do the talking! The celebrated people get headline recognition, so when we celebrate each other's achievements and success, promoting one another, we also celebrate the diversity and uniqueness of our God-given identity. Where there is favour, more follows. In a world where identity has taken centre stage on most platforms, my platforms - personal and business - challenge the true meaning and source of the concept of identity. Our business platform should reflect our best Kingdom identity because we are ambassadors of another realm. There should be no difference between private and public regarding integrity. I believe that life is about who we are, and for what purpose we were designed. To genuinely respect ourselves and to honour and respect one another is to recognise ourselves as children of God. In so doing, we honour God. All mankind is made in His image, not just followers of The Way. In a materialistic world, a coaching business that encourages self-improvement and self-discovery, not the accumulation of stuff or self-gratification through addictions that cost a small fortune, often our health or life, shines like a beacon amidst the adverts and click-bait in shops and media. It's the right time to stand up and be counted, to pin our true colors to the proverbial

Integrity - Who's Going to Know?

mast, and to stand out in a loud marketplace. Lady Wisdom stands on the street corner and shouts, "Buy my wares!"

"Wisdom shouts in the street, she lifts her voice in the square; At the head of the noisy streets she cries out; At the entrance of the gates in the city, she utters her sayings: "How long, O naive ones, will you love being simple-minded? And scoffers delight themselves in scoffing, and fools hate knowledge. "Turn to my reproof, Behold, I will pour out my spirit on you; I will make my words known to you Listen! Wisdom is calling out in the streets and marketplaces." - Proverbs 1:20, GNT

Throughout the Word of God, honour is a repeating theme. A business model that honours others through integrity gets back to a common desire and belief there must be some good people out there somewhere. I have been "bitten" by glossy adverts, and beguiled by an offer that seems "too good to be true" only to find out it was all smoke and mirrors. I've also been good to others, honest and moral, yet they've responded less than favourably. The world needs businesses run by those Kingdom-guided moral principles built on a foundation of respect for others. We must start with ourselves and work outwards!

Throughout my time as a conveyer of truth through storytelling and inspirational speaking, I have discovered a secret ingredient in my writing- the double check, which is editing- not that I always get it right! After a few edits, I always re-read it to see if it could cause harm or cause a person to be judged. In this way, I'm making sure that I am not harming one of God's children, the humans He made in His image, the people in my sphere of influence. I want to honour God. By doing this more often, I have discovered I'm learning a skill in an area in which I lacked this discernment. My speaking off the cuff! In other words- *unfiltered, uneditable, once-you've-spoken-it-you-can't-take-it-back* talking. I have learnt about honouring the gift and opportunity that God has given me. I've learned how honesty is not always the best policy, but integrity is 100% vital in gaining trust and garnering a reputation that stems from the cultivation of Kingdom principles. In relation to business, this translates into cultivating an attitude of honesty, morality, kindness, and respect, which in turn displays integrity. *Who wouldn't gravitate to that?* As a representative of the King of Kings, it is vital to the Kingdom and the success of your business that customers/clients feel you can be trusted.

Integrity - Who's Going to Know?

I have learned to not say I will definitely commit to something if anything at all can interfere with the desired outcome, and mostly in today's hectic lifestyles, there are a myriad of possible interferences. It is better to be morally upstanding and honourable which is an aspect of integrity. If we create a break of trust through raised expectations that are dashed or if we are often late, we become known as unreliable, a character that you don't want when running a business. As an example: If I plan to meet somebody over two hours away and was unable to get there early enough to be ahead of time, I wouldn't say *I will be there at 2:00 p.m."*. I would say *"I will aim to be there between 2:00 p.m. and 4:00 p.m."* Additionally, I would make sure they are contactable, if there have been unavoidable delays. This goes both ways which shows grace towards the person or people with whom you are connecting. Try different ways to assure them of your intent such as letting them know what you are doing may not happen precisely at a certain time.

If you are meeting over the internet using your computer or laptop, ensure you have a backup plan, such as a mobile device with a hotspot in case your internet goes down, your battery dies, or there's a power outage. If you've said you will be there, then be there! Yes, you are not responsible for some of these unexpected things, but you do hold a responsibility to show up! My advice here? Integrity is from the same root as integrated and integral, so ensure you put in buffers to account for the unexpected.

Another point to consider is about raising people's expectations. If you create a scenario, you are duty-bound to fulfil it. If you raise someone's expectations to a standard greater than what you can meet, both parties are disappointed. Honesty is always the best policy, even if seeming vague or unspecific feels awkward. It will be much more so if there is a failure to build a meaningful connection with a customer/client or if you bring dishonour to God by being a poor representative. To err is human, but in His Word, it says, "Bad company corrupts good character" (1 Corinthians 15:33-34, NKJV). Though it wasn't meant in this aspect, who wants to become renowned as bad company and get a name for being of dubious or unreliable character?

HONESTY REALLY IS THE BEST POLICY.

As I've crafted this chapter, it's helped me to clarify and take an honest review of my own insecurities, errors, and shortfalls. I don't feel at all knocked back by it, on the contrary. When the Holy Spirit nudges us, it's always so we can become all that He's called us to be.

INTEGRITY - WHO'S GOING TO KNOW?

Have I been honest with you in my writing? I believe so! My business is currently paused due to unavoidable personal challenges, though it may well be running again by the time this book is published! I felt a little unsure of how to convey the truth, by being honest about where I currently am with the business, but integrity is about applying moral principles with honesty so I can't mislead you into believing I have a functioning business at the time of this writing. However, I do have everything in place. That, through honour and respect as one who is living by values and moral principles, comprising of beliefs, ethics, and standards, the business is indeed exactly that. A business.

I have applied these in theory regarding my business ventures. Practically, I've applied them to the very design, framework, and modality of the business. I hope and pray this has blessed you as much as it has me. May your Kingdom business prosper and integrity guide you. May the Lord God uphold you in your integrity and set you before His face forever (application of Psalm 41:12).

ABOUT THE AUTHOR

Elizabeth worked in retail management for over twelve years until becoming a full-time homemaker. Ten years of homemaking and following divorce she was plunged into a hectic schedule of three part-time jobs and being a single mum. As a founding member of a house church, she ministered as a youth leader, preacher, teacher, and worship leader organising local events. She moved to the southwest coast of England after this abusive marriage and married again. Her 4th child, born with Trisomy 18, led to advocating for parents of disabled children in the voluntary sector forum for many years, helping to inform charters (a document outlining rights and privileges) and legislation (law-making). She has been a headline speaker at the Houses of Parliament, the Royal Banqueting Hall in London, U.K., on local radio stations, and on national television.

A three-time cancer survivor/thriver, again experiencing marital sexual abuse in her second marriage. Her experiences would envision her to instill resilience in others. Having also recently suffered child loss, homelessness, and divorce she has authored a book *EESHA - No More Silent Tears: Breaking the Silence of Marital Abuse, Restoring Hope*, and is going on to design an awareness course for ministry leaders, as well as a safe platform for victims of marital abuse. Life Without Limits is a coaching and teaching business that offers a client-led platform of self-discovery.

To Connect with Elizabeth:

mailto:lifewithoutlimits1926@gmail.com

YouTube: Eeek...let's talk

Twitter: @EeekElizabeth

Facebook: Elizabeth Kirsten

WhatsApp: +44 7787 522339

Other Books: *EESHA-No More Silent Tears*

CHAPTER 9

Gratitude Unleashed

Sonja Christine, USA
SELF-PERCEPTION COACH

TRANSFORMING LIVES THROUGH FAVHERFUL STRATEGIES

In the heart of my entrepreneurial journey lies a narrative deeply woven with personal experiences, challenges faced and overcome, and an unyielding passion to make a difference. My venture began with a fire ignited within me, fueled by a burning desire to assist those who find themselves burdened by the complexities of life. Specifically, my business focuses on professionals in the workplace - mainly women, who navigate the challenging path of parenthood alone, struggling with feelings of isolation and overwhelm.

The beginning of this adventure is rooted in my own story. After a decade spent as a single mom and a seasoned business professional, I intimately understand the struggles faced by those treading the path without the presence of a partner. This isn't just a business for me; it's a calling born out of firsthand knowledge and empathy. Growing up under the care of a single mom, I navigated through the challenges and victories inherent in this upbringing. Viewing life through the eyes of a child offers a distinctive vantage point, granting valuable insights into the complex realities faced by a single parent.

The passion that drives my initiative is a genuine, raw emotion stemming from my desire to ease the burdens of single parents who find themselves in similar circumstances. Having experienced the struggles of single motherhood as a child and as an adult, I am not only empathetic but resilient. My triumphs fuel my determination to extend hope and guidance to those who feel alone and burnt out.

Beyond my personal history, I also recognize the universal struggles faced by single dads. The inclusivity of my initiative reflects a deep understanding of diverse experiences and a commitment to addressing the needs of all individuals navigating the challenges of single parenthood. It's not just about business — it's about creating a community, promoting connections, and providing a support system with accountability for those who feel isolated.

My motivation is to make a meaningful impact on people's lives. Trauma, a silent companion on the journey of life, is recognized as a force that can significantly and profoundly shape an individual. I confronted personal traumas and realized the importance of healing and the transformative power of self-love.

My passion for this endeavor is to be a beacon that shines brightly, guiding others toward a path of self-discovery, healing, and love. My journey from not knowing what real love and relationships were, to cultivating a deep connection with God by understanding my identity in Him, forms the foundation of the services I offer.

In a world that often seems to lack compassion and understanding, my initiative stands as a testament to the belief that the world needs love. By sharing my personal experiences, nurturing self-love, and developing meaningful connections, I aim to create a ripple effect that goes beyond individual lives and dominates the world with compassion, understanding, and hope for a bright future.

Within my business, FavHERful Strategies, I possess the ability to unveil in other's aspects of themselves that remained buried in walls built by trauma. I guide individuals to revisit their dreams, facilitating an exploration of why they have deviated from their initial path or helping them envision an alternative perspective where their aspirations can manifest. Through a supportive process, I aid clients in mapping out the life they desire fostering a deep understanding of their worth. As part of this transformative journey, I provide them with affirmations that reinforce their self-love and acknowledge their accomplishments. Moreover, I encourage gratitude for the positive aspects of their journey, but also include the challenges, recognizing that both contribute to their growth and resilience. Clients embracing gratitude for both the good and the seemingly difficult learn to love themselves and gain insight into their life achievements discovering the hope and empowerment needed to alter their course, if deemed necessary.

The Kingdom principle of gratitude takes on a deeper dimension when applied to challenges and setbacks, offering resilience and a powerful antidote to anxiety. Instead of viewing challenges as insurmountable obstacles, individuals are encouraged to see them as opportunities for growth—a shift that aligns with the biblical principle of finding strength in adversity. As clients develop gratitude amidst difficulties, they alleviate burdens of anxiety by shifting their focus from the challenges they face to the things they are grateful for. This shift in perspective helps them cultivate a positive mindset, which can reduce feelings of stress and overwhelm. This intentional practice of gratitude becomes a powerful resilience-building tool, empowering individuals to navigate life's challenges with a mindset deeply rooted in self-love and acceptance. Moreover, the act of appreciating the positive aspects of their journey, even when faced with challenges, fosters a sense of calm and assurance that they have the inner resources to overcome obstacles.

In the realm of coaching, integrating Kingdom principles, particularly the virtue of gratitude, is a transformative force that elevates individual growth. Gratitude goes beyond an expression of thankfulness; it becomes a guiding light that brightens the path to self-discovery and mind transformation. It's a deep-rooted acknowledgment of the blessings, both seen and unseen, that spreads throughout every aspect of life. Building a culture where being thankful goes beyond just feeling happy for a moment is important. Adding gratitude on purpose helps make significant changes in your life thus impacting those around you. Coaches are like guides who help people think about themselves and appreciate what makes them special. We encourage folks to see their strengths and how they handle tough times, starting them on a path to being kind to themselves. This journey leads individuals to a point when a shift occurs—a transformative moment where perspectives are flipped to perceive the positive in every aspect of life. Drawing inspiration from the biblical wisdom found in Romans 12:2, individuals are reminded not to conform to the patterns of the world but to undergo a metamorphosis through the renewal of their minds. This renewal is not simply a cognitive shift; it is a holistic transformation that empowers individuals to discern and embrace the goodness, acceptability, and perfection in the divine will of God.

Incorporating the principles of gratitude into relationships and personal connections resonates deeply with the foundational teachings of the Bible, as articulated in Mark 12:30-31: "And you shall love the Lord your God with all your heart, with all your soul, with all your mind, and with all your strength. This is the first commandment. And the second, like it, is this: 'You shall love your neighbor as yourself.' There is no other commandment greater than these" (NKJV). This guidance underscores the significance of actively promoting gratitude in the context of loving one's neighbor as oneself. When coaches and speakers actively encourage the expression of gratitude towards those who have positively impacted their clients' lives, they embody the essence of these commandments. This intentional practice becomes a conduit for strengthening interpersonal bonds, fostering a deep profound sense of unity and harmony among individuals. As client's express gratitude for the positive roles played by others, they not only acknowledge the interconnectedness woven into their respective journeys toward self-love but also reflect the divine commandments to love God with all their being and to love their neighbors as themselves.

Gratitude in a Corporate World

In an age when the unyielding quest for profit and shareholder value frequently shape the corporate environment, businesses like mine, firmly grounded in Kingdom principles, rise as beacons illuminating a distinctive paradigm. This framework is deeply rooted in values that transcend mere financial concerns. What distinguishes these businesses extends beyond their products or services; it's the pervasive influence of principled guidance, centered on God and nurturing relationships with people, that infuses every aspect of operations. Kingdom businesses shine as advocates for a more profound and conscientious approach. Embracing and implementing Kingdom principles in my business goes beyond being a mere strategy; it's a lifestyle.

With gratitude as the foundation, this way of life involves being mindful of your thoughts and promotes a mindset that recognizes and appreciates the positive aspects of every undertaking.

Expressing gratitude for challenges and opportunities often viewed negatively by others, triggers a positive mindset shift, resulting in more favorable outcomes. In my career working at a Global IT outsourcing company, I was a project manager for several Fortune 500 companies. I oversaw transitions and transformations within the organizations. This included implementing new or upgrading existing services along with any other change to an organization's technology. These activities brought many challenges with tools, people, and processes. Instead of dwelling on negativity, I concentrated on finding solutions with optimism utilizing relationships I built over time. I prayed for the company, my team, and the necessary work, seeking divine strategies for our project's success. I expressed gratitude to my team and my clients. Guided by the principle in 1 Thessalonians 5:16-18, "Rejoice always, pray without ceasing, in everything give thanks; for this is the will of God in Christ Jesus for you" (NKJV), this positive approach enabled effective collaboration, leveraging team strengths to overcome issues. These experiences led to resolutions and contributed to my personal growth.

This gratitude-centered approach shapes decision-making, actions, and interactions, establishing business values rooted in lasting client and employee relationships. Building a culture where being thankful goes beyond just feeling happy for a moment is important. Adding gratitude on purpose helps make significant changes in your life thus positively impacting everyone around you.

By incorporating gratitude into the decision-making process in any business, we recognize and appreciate the invaluable contributions of our stakeholders and the communities we serve. Gratitude influences our approach by fostering a deep sense of appreciation for the well-being of individuals and communities we serve. This perspective guides us to prioritize the holistic welfare of our employees, customers, and society as a whole, rather than solely focusing on profit-driven objectives. By expressing gratitude for the trust and support bestowed upon us, we aim to create a business environment rooted in compassion, integrity, and mutual respect. This not only enhances the professional and personal lives of our stakeholders but also strengthens the bonds within our community. Gratitude inspires us to actively engage in initiatives that uplift and support those in need, reinforcing our commitment to making a positive impact beyond financial success. Gratitude serves as a guiding principle that shapes our business practices, reminding us that true prosperity is achieved through the collective well-being of all those we touch.

Fostering a Gratitude Community

The impact of gratitude extends beyond individual coaching sessions. Creating a community where clients can share their gratitude experiences, insights, and challenges fosters a supportive network. This communal aspect further strengthens the Kingdom principle of interconnectedness creating a dynamic environment where individuals draw inspiration from each other's journeys. It goes beyond inspiration, fostering a space that provides hope and accountability through encouragement, support, and a shared sense of purpose. In this community, individuals find solace in shared experiences, celebrate victories together, and offer compassion during challenges. It becomes a source of empowerment, camaraderie, and spiritual nourishment, enhancing the transformative impact of the interconnectedness principle.

Embracing the Kingdom principle of gratitude can remarkably impact both personal and professional lives, fostering a culture of positivity and well-being.

The following are actionable tips and strategies to continuously integrate gratitude into your daily routine:

GRATITUDE JOURNALING

Initiate a gratitude journaling routine, dedicating a few moments each day to record three things you are thankful for. Whether it's a modest achievement, a fleeting moment of joy, or the comforting warmth of sunshine, this practice serves to instill a habit of recognizing and cherishing the positive elements in your life. If you are already engaged in journaling, seamlessly incorporate these daily expressions of gratitude to enhance your reflective practice.

MINDFUL APPRECIATION

Bring mindfulness into your gratitude routine. Spend a few moments each day thinking about and appreciating what's happening around you. This makes your gratitude more special, letting you enjoy and feel the good things in your life. To kick off your day, write down three things you're grateful for, such as the warmth of a blanket, the friendly notes your barista adds to your coffee, and the beautiful rainbow that reminds you of God's promises. Doing this in the morning helps your brain start the day on a positive note. Challenge yourself to think of different things each day, but also give yourself some grace on the days that it's harder. When life gets tough, going back to read what you have written is a helpful way to shift your perspective.

Family Gratitude Rituals

Extend the practice of gratitude to your family life. Create a routine where each family member shares three things they are grateful for that day. This could be during a car ride or at a meal shared. Encourage even the smallest expressions of gratitude, such as appreciating a meal, a toy, a beloved pet, a friend, a bed, or the presence of family members. After a week or two, encourage them to think about more meaningful things, such as the teacher who may be strict but supports them every day or the important role of bees in pollinating flowers and making honey. Make sure the example topics are suitable for their age.

Here Are Some Others To Consider

- Thanking people who have been kind or helpful.
- Appreciating the fun provided by age-appropriate technology. Parents can be grateful for the learning opportunities it provides their children.
- Being thankful for meals to nourish their bodies.
- Being able to play sports or go to concerts.

Thank You Notes

Reintroduce the charm of handwritten thank you notes. Send notes of appreciation to colleagues, clients, or family members. The personal touch of a handwritten note adds sincerity and can leave a lasting impression.

Personal to a Friend Example

Dear [Recipient's Name],

I just wanted to take a few minutes and let you know how truly thankful I am for your support and kindness. Having you as a [friend/mentor] has had a positive impact on me. Your positive influence has made a difference in my life. Thanks for always being there to help me out. I appreciate everything you've done.

[Kind Regards/Love/Blessings],
[Your Name]

Express Gratitude To Team Members

In a business setting, make expressing gratitude to your team a regular practice. Acknowledge their efforts, accomplishments, and positive contributions. This boosts morale and creates a collaborative and supportive work environment.

Express Gratitude Among Team Members

Express appreciation by upholding clear and honest communication channels, enabling team members to openly express their thoughts and concerns. Encourage the collaboration of their peers to include positive feedback around the people, processes, and tools they are working with daily. Use a collaboration tool within your company such as Teams or Slack to set up a channel just for gratitude. Have a challenge for your team to help come up with what works best for them. If they are included in building the process, they are more likely to use it.

NOTE: IT'S IMPORTANT TO ESTABLISH BOUNDARIES FOR THIS TO PREVENT IT FROM TURNING INTO A PLATFORM FOR VENTING OR BASHING.

Client Appreciation

Extend gratitude to your clients for their trust and partnership. Regularly express thanks through personalized notes or some way of appreciation. This strengthens client relationships and fosters a positive reputation for your business.

Professional to Client Example

Dear [Client's Name],
I wanted to take a moment to express my sincere gratitude for your trust and partnership. Your confidence in our services means a great deal to us, and we truly appreciate the opportunity to work with you. Your collaboration has been invaluable, and we are thankful for the positive relationship we've built together. We look forward to continuing to meet your needs and exceed your expectations. Thank you once again for choosing us as your partner. We value your business and the trust you've placed in our team.

Best Regards,

[Your Name]
[Your Position]
[Your Company]

GRATITUDE CHALLENGES

Create a fun and healthy way of encouraging gratitude within your family or team. Set weekly goals for expressing gratitude, encouraging everyone to participate actively. This can instill a sense of healthy competition and deepen the collective commitment to gratitude.

The Gratitude Challenge Game

- <u>OBJECTIVE:</u> Encourage participants to set weekly gratitude goals and engage in a fun game to achieve them.
- <u>INSTRUCTIONS:</u> At the beginning of each week, participants set three specific gratitude goals for the week. These goals can be related to recognizing positive aspects in various areas of life, expressing thanks, or fostering a grateful mindset.
- <u>GRATITUDE POINTS:</u> Assign points to different gratitude-related activities. For example:
    - 5 points for expressing gratitude to a friend or family member.
    - 10 points for recognizing and appreciating a colleague's efforts at work.
    - 15 points for writing down three things they are grateful for each day.
    - Additionally, award 1 extra point for every gratitude entry beyond the initial three.
- <u>TRACKING:</u> Participants keep track of their points throughout the week by recording completed activities on a gratitude challenge sheet.
- <u>Weekly Review</u>: At the end of the week, gather participants and discuss their experiences. Ask them to share which activities were the most impactful and why. Recognize and celebrate individual or collective achievements.

- <u>PRIZES OR RECOGNITION:</u> Consider offering small rewards or recognition for participants who consistently engage in gratitude activities and meet their weekly goals. It could be as easy as a Gratitude Gem. You can find a shiny rock or gem to give to the winner each week or print out a Gratitude Gem award. Alternatively, you can make a cardboard one together as a family activity and display it for that family member each week.

For corporate settings, have employees include it in their email signature or come up with a way for them to be recognized as the *Gratitude Gem*. Ask your executive management to support it and spark a company initiative, *"Gratitude Ripple Effect."* This gratitude challenge game combines goal-setting with a point system to make the practice of gratitude interactive and enjoyable. It encourages participants to actively seek and acknowledge positive aspects in their lives.

Gratitude Workshops or Seminars

Consider organizing workshops or seminars on gratitude for your team. Invite experts, such as counselors or life coaches, to share insights on the benefits of gratitude. This educational component can deepen understanding and commitment to integrating gratitude into daily life.

Gratitude Unleashed

Gratitude Challenges on Social Media

Leverage the power of social media to spread gratitude. Inspire a positive online community by prompting individuals to share what they're thankful for.

Here Are Some Examples:

- "What are you grateful for? Mine is in the comments." Set an example and post what you are thankful for in your comments.
- Show me a photo of what you are grateful for. Post yours for attention to the post.
- "What's the best thing to happen to you last week?" I encourage you to brag!

Embrace negativity as an opportunity to redirect the narrative with resilience and positivity. Every comment is a chance to turn the conversation toward gratitude and kindness. Consistency is key when integrating gratitude into your life and business. By incorporating these practices into your daily routine, you cultivate a personal sense of well-being and contribute to creating a positive and thriving environment in your family and workplace. Remember, gratitude is a powerful force when embraced with the potential to transform both individual lives and the dynamics of an entire business community.

In the realm of Kingdom business, where principles of integrity, compassion and service with gratitude form the cornerstone, there emerges a beacon of light challenging the conventional norms of profit-driven enterprises. This business framework, deeply entwined with kingdom principles, emphasizes purpose-driven endeavors over mere financial gains. It's a call to businesses to thrive economically and contribute to the holistic well-being of individuals and communities. It becomes evident that the integration of these principles has the potential to spark transformative change in our world.

From gratitude journals to family rituals and expressions of thanks within a team or client interactions, the practice of gratitude becomes a transformative thread woven into the very fabric of daily life. It's not just a positive sentiment but a powerful tool that shapes perspectives, fosters resilience, and reduces anxiety. The ripple effect of these principles extends beyond individual lives.

We can envision a world where businesses are not solely focused on profit margins but are actively engaged in nurturing the well-being of individuals and communities. It paints a picture of societies where self-love is not a luxury but a foundational principle, leading to healthier relationships, thriving communities, and a collective shift towards a more compassionate and purpose-driven existence.

In essence, the harmony of Kingdom principles with the journey of self-love creates a joint operation capable of rewriting the narrative of our world. It's a call to action, urging individuals and businesses alike to embody these principles, not just for personal fulfillment but as a collective endeavor to create a world where love, purpose, and compassion tower above. As we move forward, let these principles guide our decisions, actions, and interactions, paving the way for a positive, brighter, and more harmonious future.

ABOUT THE AUTHOR

Meet Sonja Christine, a resilient single mom in her 40s who navigated a remarkable journey from a two-decade-long career in IT to becoming a beacon of inspiration for others. With over 20 years of expertise in the dynamic field of Information Technology, she seamlessly transitioned her professional acumen into a personal life map for success and transformation.

In the face of life's challenges, Sonja courageously embraced change, turning her experiences into stepping-stones rather than stumbling blocks. As a single mother, she defied the odds, leveraging her IT and project management background to engineer a powerful transformation in her life.

Driven by a passion for empowerment and growth, Sonja has meticulously crafted a life map to success program based on her own life's journey. Now, she is on a mission to share this invaluable guide with the world, offering insights, strategies, and a reservoir of wisdom garnered from her metamorphosis.

Currently, Sonja is writing another book, delving into her journey of self-love through a relationship with God and how it has been the cornerstone of her life's transformation. Through her forthcoming book, she aims to inspire others to embark on their journey of self-discovery and love. Join Sonja on her empowering odyssey as she lights the way for others to discover their avenues of transformation and success.

TO CONNECT WITH SONJA:

Linked In - linkedin.com/in/sonjasams
Facebook - facebook.com/snydersams
Website - https://www.sonjachristine.com/

CHAPTER 10

A Spirit of Gratitude

Nestor Gomez, USA
PASTOR AND MOTIVATIONAL SPEAKER

Over the years, I have seen the need in my Latin American community to advance knowledge about economic success. I decided to help my community understand biblical principles in the area of finances through workshops, conferences, and sermons. It has always been a challenge to see a community continuously emerge in a new sphere of the world; in a new environment making history in the country that embraced, welcomed, and adopted us- the United States of America.

The American dream is still a dream for many people, perhaps a fantasy or unattainable possibility, the difference between day and night. Many interrupt the breezes, the rains, and the snows of the seasons to work incessantly seeking to obtain that elusive American dream. With hearts broken into several pieces between "the over here" and "the over there" - the place where we now find ourselves, this beautiful American nation and the land of our childhood, family, and places we left behind which seemed to no longer exist, the American dream, proclaimed and even glorified can be achieved, if the objective is having a home, a job, and stability. But for too many, the American dream is to escape the terror that overwhelmed them in their nation of origin and live in a nation where their freedoms are respected in some way.

My observation of the Anglo culture leads me to think they define that same dream as the power of achievement, economic stability, and educational achievement, believing that these bring family satisfaction because they have more than enough. I do not doubt this is a good expectation, however, I believe the American dream becomes a fallacy - a mistaken belief - when after achieving all its expectations, people can still find themselves with a void they cannot fill or satisfy which in turn requires them to need more and more to feel fulfilled and declare out loud, "I have fulfilled the American dream."

Now, don't think that I am against achieving all your goals and achieving everything you want. For me, success is when you not only have what you want but also being happy with who you are. When we discover who we are, we allow what we have to be used for who we are; that is where we find the reality of purpose which is true success and the perfect explanation of the American dream. This should be the objective of every Christian; to be able to fulfill the divine purpose in our lives with what we have because of who we are in Christ.

From a young age, there was a call to serve God in the work of the ministry and I responded to that call. My mother told me when I was a child, she found me preaching fervently and passionately to the chickens in a pen in my native Colombia. My mother jokingly tells me "Your first audience was chickens." I vividly remember being nine years old sitting in the pew of our congregation paying full attention to the preacher with my heart pounding a thousand minutes away. I felt that passion, that fire, inside of me. I could clearly hear my thoughts that rumbled without limit declaring, "That is what I want to do for the rest of my life!" That is precisely what I have been doing since my childhood, traveling the world, preaching the Word of God, teaching and preparing men and women with principles of the Kingdom, including the subject of finances. On this journey, God has allowed me to help companies in the organization and preparation of their staff, and I am currently the pastor of Casa Servir, a spectacular congregation that God allowed my wife and me to establish fourteen years ago, just outside of New York City.

I firmly believe that teaching and preparing people to develop their leadership abilities and to be able to work as a team while following a plan to face different challenges within their responsibilities in their corresponding companies helped me to prepare the staff and members of our congregation. Developing leadership, the ability to serve in strong teams, discovering their functional gift bringing to light how their personality is solidifying their strength in preparing them to develop healthy relationships within their homes, in their communities, and also in our congregation. I am passionate about doing what I do. It is a calling and a privilege to be able to see and collaborate with others to be able to get to where they have always wanted to go. Seeing the hand of God work with them and his presence illuminate their understanding and watch their lives transformed in this life process. As people with an eternal calling of the Kingdom of God, it's about fulfilling God's dreams in our lives, what He has planned, not about fulfilling the American dream. We can do this when we realize our gifts, skills, experiences, education, personality, passion, and values have been embedded in our being, by birth, upbringing, environment, or formal preparation.

As a pastor, I have been leading our congregation, bringing a teaching, a workshop, a sermon, a council, to communicate the principles of the Kingdom and make a difference in their lives and their families by impacting their different spheres of influence, even their friends and family in their native country. One of the principles has been giving and serving as a sign of gratitude. The reality is our actions of giving and serving are linked to an economy that extends beyond what we normally think. One of the countless examples comes to mind: one of the brothers in our congregation had several needs. He needed his legal status papers to be approved. He needed to move and get a house, then he wanted to have a child. Three specific requests. His papers had been lost in some way that had caused his immigration process to be delayed and there was no way for this to be expedited. He had been at this crossroads for a while and wanted it to progress, but these papers he needed to be approved were preventing any progress. The place where he lived made it difficult for him to be able to maintain all the tools he used to make and bring

A Spirit of Gratitude

daily bread to his family. There were other reasons why he could no longer live where he was living. His wife and two daughters needed a more spacious place, and he longed to have a son. He loved his two daughters, but he longed to have a boy, but his wife was resisting his request. I remember talking to him after he selflessly helped another family by repairing their front and back house porches and building a place to store some household tools. He told me he believed what I was teaching in those days - the principle of giving and serving as a form of gratitude and he was putting it into practice. What we were teaching the congregation motivated him to continue blessing others, and to give what he had. I prayed for him asking God to honor what this man had done, by blessing this family who desperately needed the help and did not have the resources to pay someone. A month later, his wife changed her mind and became pregnant. Nine months later, the boy is a blessing to her heart and the child looks exactly like his father. God answered him. The papers that had disappeared appeared and within 24 hours, he received a response and was able to obtain his passport to travel to his homeland to visit his family he had not seen in many years. If this was not enough, God blessed him so much that he was able to buy two houses in a period of two years. This is one of the examples I can share of how God honors the spirit of gratitude expressed in acts of service and acts of giving. That is how God works!

In a multicultural church like ours, there are more than ten different nationalities. The different personalities, and cultural, educational, and doctrinal backgrounds bring different challenges and give me a platform to sow transformative principles and watch how, little by little, as a seed planted in a field in time, after being cared for and nourished, produces its fruit. I observe how people who start with nothing progress in an incredible way, so even they are in a state of awe and gratitude as they enjoy the fruit of practicing Kingdom principles; all because they have been able to come to understand principles of dedication and effort, especially those who understand the purpose for which God blesses us and gives us opportunities and responsibilities.

I hear the excited voice accompanied by an explosive smile and with giant steps hurry to stop me in one of the corridors of the temple. It is a man in the church who approaches me to tell me, "Pastor, we have moved from the room where we lived in a house where different rooms were rented. We are no longer afraid of living in one room, having to share the bathroom, the kitchen, and the rest of the house with other families. At last, we have privacy! Thank

A SPIRIT OF GRATITUDE

you, pastor, for teaching me the principles of Kingdom." I can tell you one story after another of how I have seen people in our congregation arrive with nothing but their dreams and desires to be able to see the materialization and realization of those dreams and desires. Not in vain through these years, it has been the effort and time invested in people whom God has allowed me and my wife to minister to with the principles of the Kingdom including the principles relating to finance.

"You will be enriched in every way for your great generosity, which will produce thanksgiving to God through us. For the rendering of this ministry not only supplies the needs of the saints but also overflows with many thanksgivings to God. - 2 Corinthians 9:11-12, NRSV

In this scripture, we see how the apostle Paul is stating that the believers in Macedonia would be receiving a generous offering from the congregation that was in Corinth, whose offering they had to prepare in advance. In this biblical text and its context, we clearly see three words I have been sharing with you in this chapter are perfectly linked: generosity, service, and thanksgiving.

The apostle Paul emphasizes to us that the offerings they have collected must serve these brothers in faith who come from Macedonia, and this comes from a gesture of generosity on the part of the believers of the church of Corinth. The fact that they gather these offerings and the dedication to giving them to these brothers from Macedonia is an act of service that must produce gratitude and praise in the one who is blessed, the one who receives the offerings. They glorify God, who is the spirit of gratitude that arises from an act of obedience operating in a spirit of generosity based on what we have - finances, material things, possessions, resources, and efforts of those who decide to give. Notice that verse twelve emphasizes not only the benefit of meeting a need for something that is materially lacking in the Macedonian believers but also leads to thanksgiving in those who were in need.

I am a pastor. I am a minister of the Lord. It is my duty to bring the congregation to a safe harbor with the help of Our Lord Jesus Christ and His Holy Spirit. A safe harbor is available to all those who are open to being taught and learning how to use what God has placed in their hands. By being an instrument of glory and praise to God through the administration of their body, talents, family, work, ministry, and community service, using the positions and money God allows them to earn by creating the human being, their life, their personality, and their free will to take the road to the harbor of complete freedom.

A Spirit of Gratitude

Let me share with you, scripturally, what God the Father has been teaching me about the spirit of gratitude. I cannot cover all the scriptures that exist about gratitude or all the truths that can be expressed on this subject. I am writing a whole book on this topic but want to tell you a couple of details that sometimes may go unnoticed.

First, let me define the word *thanksgiving* in the New Testament. The Greek word we find in the New Testament is εὐχαριστία (eucharistia), and where we get the word eucharist. According to the Strong's Concordance: thankfulness, gratitude; giving of thanks, thanksgiving, gratitude; actively, grateful language (to God, as an act of worship).

God Owns My Thanksgiving

"And all the angels stood round about the throne, and about the elders and the four living beings, and fell on their faces before the throne and worshiped God, saying, "Amen. Blessing and glory and wisdom and thanksgiving, and honor and power and might, be unto our God forever and ever. Amen!" - Revelation 7:11-12, KJ21

"And when those living beings give glory and honor and thanks to Him that sat on the throne, who liveth forever and ever." - Revelation 4:9, KJ21

We can see that thanksgiving is something that is active, and that if it is an act of praise of acknowledgment, it is an action given to someone outside of ourselves, in this case to God.

Second, let us consider the principle of gratitude. There is an abundance of insights and opinions about being grateful. We have been told about expressing gratitude to our loved ones, to those who work with us, and to those people with whom we have interactions within daily life. We also need to understand that thanksgiving begins by being grateful to God.

One cannot begin to speak of gratitude and not put God in the circle. To place God outside of the gratitude a human being must possess is to ignore that He is the creator. Not only of the physiological or intellectual body of man or woman but also of the internal laws and principles our bodies carry internally. I believe mankind should be taught to express gratitude because it is already in the spirit of man as a result of being created by God. In the same way, He fits within us what we know as faith, God resides in us with the spirit of gratitude. It is there as if sleeping, waiting to be exercised, fed, and developed so that it can express itself and come to light with our words and actions. We can express gratitude because we are the image and likeness of

A Spirit of Gratitude

God. He celebrates what He creates, does, moves, and arranges. He celebrates His creation and in that same image and likeness, there is the spirit of gratitude. It is linked to the spirit of celebration, to the spirit of humility, and God, our heavenly Father, is embodied in the life of Jesus Christ and in the manifestation of the Holy Spirit. In Jesus, we see the spirit who celebrates, is humble, and is grateful, and in the Holy Spirit, we witness the same manner in the sacred scripture (the Bible).

Celebrating with humility is a result of our faith in God, therefore we have to make decisions that produce celebration. One of the ways we can do that is by expressing our generosity with our finances and resources then others can also celebrate by being beneficiaries of the blessings received from God through us. At the same time, we can celebrate our prosperity because we have the ability to be blessed to bless others. This is like a continuous cause and effect. Our economy is linked to the resources, talents, opportunities, sacrifices, disposition, knowledge, preparation, and administration we possess, of what we undertake and have. As believers, we do all this depending on an attitude of faith in God who guides our steps, recognizing that He is the giver of what we have by birth in our being and of what we acquire through what God has already given us. It is undoubtedly connected to the call to express gratitude to God before obtaining our financial success and continues beyond to all spheres of our lives. Our gratitude continually grows because we see how God blesses us and we understand how much we actually have and don't realize it, so we find ourselves in endless gratitude. Think for a moment about people who cannot enjoy their financial prosperity and bitterness controls their hearts full of anxiety, not because they lack something material but because their spirit cannot enjoy what they have. A dose of gratitude would warm their heart and help them enjoy what they have.

God owns our thanksgiving and expressions of thanksgiving as a token of adoration and worship Him for showing His grace to us. Thanksgiving is part of God's seven acknowledgments and perfect confessions. The Scriptures clearly declaring to us that God owns thanksgiving. We see how the angels around His throne are declaring a powerful confession where it includes thankfulness, they are saying: *"There can be no thankfulness apart from you our God, for You are the origin of everything."* Why is this important? Because it binds us, connects us, and unites us with our origin, God. He operates in us and everything we do must have a reciprocal effect towards God on our part. It is our actions and words of gratitude that are part of God's seven acknowledgments and perfect confessions as I call them.

This thanksgiving is acknowledging the authority of God, the supremacy of God, the uniqueness of God. In the Bible, you will find it begins with the top of the head to reach the soles of the feet. This is how the anointing begins. This is how praise is manifested. This is how respect is taught. This is how thanksgiving is shown. As Christians, our thankfulness begins in God, then is extended to the body He in Christ formed, the church, then it pours out on the world that He loves and who needs Him desperately and ends where it began: in Him God of the universe and all.

It's What God Wants Us To Do All The Time And For Everything

It is so important to God that we give thanks to Him not only because He is the owner of our thanks, as I have explained, but as the Creator also knows that it is a benefit for us as people, in our emotions, in our thoughts, in our health, which also affects our attitude and aptitude and even our way of seeing life. At the same time, our gratitude must be acted upon, given in the Name of our Lord Jesus Christ, as an endorsement of what we have received, what we have lived, and what we have done, is linked to His help, for He is involved in everything that has to do with us; For if we say that we are His and He is our Lord, we are declaring that as the owner of us we cannot do anything that we can do. It is in His name we thank God because His name represents His reputation, it reveals the action that He does in, by, and through us whether visible or invisible. The name of Christ, accompanied by faith, is the key and the door that gives access to the Father.

The Holy Scripture says it clearly: "In everything give thanks, for this is the will of God in Christ Jesus concerning you." - 1 Thessalonians 5:18, KJ21

"Giving thanks always for all things unto God and the Father in the name of our Lord Jesus Christ." -Ephesians 5:20, KJ21

The question then becomes: what do I do now? How can I take this principle of thankfulness to God and bring it into my life, into my business, into my family, into the church that I belong to, and into the relationships I am in?

First, start with acknowledging your lack of gratitude to God. Take the time to examine your action: Are you truly expressing actively, continuously, in detail, sincere thanks to God?

Second, be specific and ask God's forgiveness, if you have the conviction that you have failed in this area by not living a grateful life with your creator.

Third, start being intentionally thoughtful with God; express yourself in your own words for what

A Spirit of Gratitude

and why you are thanking Him. Take the time to think about yourself when you talk to Him, use your own language, and express your feelings and thoughts, you do not have to imitate anyone else.

Fourth, you must be convinced that thanksgiving belongs to God because He is your creator, if God is not your personal God, then your thanksgiving will not be either.

Fifth, be clear and accept that God wants you to thank Him and to do so using the name of Jesus Christ because even if you don't know it or see it, Jesus is involved in your responses, benefits, and triumphs, and even in the adverse and difficult moments in your life.

Sixth, begin and end everything you do with expressions and actions of gratitude toward God, as another way to worship God.

Seventh, apply this principle of expressing gratitude to other people because the benefit to all areas of your life will be immensely positive. The Creator tells you to give thanks for everything. You begin and end your day by thanking, not only God but those who interact with you. Have you ever heard that phrase that the one who sings prays twice? I dare say the one who expresses gratitude praises God twice. God shows His grace to us then we express our gratitude to Him.

More than recycling, it is the favorable action of God to our lives, which we recognize and identify, and once we assimilate it within us, we have the conviction that we cannot take possession of that immense favor of God towards us, that we have to turn them into thanksgiving. This circle that begins at the top passes through us and ends at the top on the very throne of God. Generating beneficial consequences in every area of our lives, doesn't this seem like a spectacular and ingenious formula of our Supreme Creator? I always say, "God deals with 1000 things with one stone."

More Bible texts and other principles around gratitude are being prepared for one of my books to be released in the near future, but I wanted to emphasize this foundational principle: God is the owner of our thanksgiving and is the basis of every principle that derives from thanksgiving. If we do not begin there, we will not be able to end with thanksgivings that are entrenched in God, where you belong. If God is not present as the reason, the motivation, and the essence of our thanksgiving, not only to Him but to every other person, regardless of whether they are Christian or not, then they are simply formal, polite, spiritless words.

I encourage you to begin your day on God's throne of grace with actions of gratitude and come out of

A Spirit of Gratitude

there ready to impact lives who can see in you someone grateful, whose cordiality knows perspires the glory of God, and I do not doubt this causes others to be interested not only in you but in whom you represent, "the owner of your thanksgiving."

ABOUT THE AUTHOR

Rev. Nestor Gómez Freja was born in Colombia and has served our Lord Jesus Christ since the age of nine, came to the United States to participate in events organized by the Billy Graham Evangelistic Association. He was called from an early age to the ministry and has collaborated with different organizations in different Latin American countries, allowing him to work in the missionary, pastoral, and evangelistic work among children, young people, and adults for the last forty-five years. His experience as a marketing manager in the health area for several years has allowed him to have a more comprehensive balance when it comes to being a mentor and coach in the secular sphere. He has a degree in theology from the Biblical Seminary of Colombia, has received formal training in the area of leadership and pastoral care, and is also a trainer for Christian and secular companies preparing their personnel.

He has written and prepared a series of workshop manuals aimed at service and teamwork, leadership training, functioning according to spiritual gifts, and the effectiveness of service inside and outside the church, and is a frequently requested speaker and preacher for various Christian denominations and secular companies. At the moment Reverend Néstor Gómez Freja is in the process of publishing several books. Currently, he is pastoring with his wife, Rosa the congregation Casa Servir (house of service) in

A Spirit of Gratitude

upstate New York, whose work God allowed him to establish together with his family fourteen years ago. And he's the host of the God in Action (Dios en Accion) podcast that's heard in more than 36 countries. He and his wife are the parents of three adult children who also are serving God.

To Connect with Nestor:

Email: casaservir@yahoo.com
Facebook: facebook.com/casa.servir
facebook.com/nestor.gomezfreja
Instagram: @gomezfreja @casaservir
Podcast: Diosenaccion.com
Website: www.casaservir.com

CHAPTER 11

Authenticity
Destruction to Radical Destiny

Chris Porter, UK
PURPOSE & CONFIDENCE COACH

Radiant Destiny Coaching and Counselling Services was born out of utter emotional turmoil, rejection, and heartache. It was also birthed out of my initial response to my circumstances at that time. With hindsight, I believe the Lord was working in me to recover from the trauma and pain to help others. This gave me a reason to continue at the time when the fight for my marriage had failed and I found myself alone and grieving. My grief was not only for my marriage ending but also for my son who had stayed with my husband.

Authenticity - Destruction to Radical Destiny

I came from a stable background within a loving missionary family and married in my early twenties. Whilst a student, my parents had returned to serve abroad as missionaries. I married on completion of my degree. I had never contemplated divorce and I did not believe in it. Fast forward three decades and you would have seen my family moving me out of my home into separate accommodations with my heart breaking. I thought it was more important that my son, as a new young adult, had his Dad around him; for that reason, I was the one to move. This led to untold pain, grief, and rejection, and the need to find a way to rebuild again without my family.

October 2014 was a defining moment in many ways because I was faced with unforeseen rejection, emotional pain, which I had never experienced before, and an isolation that was unbearable. I had not lived as an adult on my own and now I was forced to learn to live alone, without family support and with anxiety about my direction and finances for the future. This traumatic break-up led me through a convoluted route to where I am today – authentically living out my destiny

I remember someone once sharing a prophetic word for me and it was about walking across on solid steppingstones to the other side. I can truly say that the Lord provided significant solid steppingstones for me along the way so that a journey that could have stunted me forever has enabled me to inspire and equip others.

A decade later through Radical Destiny Coaching & Counselling Services, I have taken pain, process, and perspectives and created my signature programme for God's VIPs; women who want to either empower women or grow themselves in their value, identity, and purpose. I have reflected on the hard experience and found an easier path.

The hard life I refer to includes heaviness, anxiety, rejection, and despair to be replaced with an easier one which involves:

- Energising sense of worth and value.
- A clear purpose.
- Sense of belonging.
- Equipping to grow in my identity in Christ.

This helps women leaders to confidently empower others or themselves to:

- Rebuild their lives after rejection and loss.
- Identify their true value and identity.
- Find and communicate authentically with themselves, others, and God.
- Find and fulfil their God-given purpose.
- Find their authentic voice and share it authentically.

Authenticity - Destruction to Radical Destiny

I have recently read the passage in Nehemiah in which God takes a man who was a slave to a foreign King and uses him to rebuild the walls of Jerusalem after he prays and fasts. Nehemiah means "Yahweh has comforted." The repair work started with God's comfort. Once we receive God's comfort, it is to be shared with others. We read in the Bible that God, "Comforteth us in all our tribulation, that we may be able to comfort those who are in any trouble by the comfort wherewith we ourselves are comforted by God" (2 Corinthians 1:4 KJV).

My own story has been one of receiving God's comfort and wanting to equip others to empower women to do the same: to "rebuild the walls." To empower women to be all they can be and shine brightly in a dark world. My signature programme, "God's VIPs," refers to value, identity and purpose and is a three-pronged approach to being able to rebuild the walls of our lives and communities and live our God-given purpose.

The framework has been created from my experience and includes:

1. Rejection initially
2. Response
3. Re-evaluation
4. Rebuilding
5. Restoration
6. Redeeming time and opportunity

I can now help professional helpers assist women who have experienced rejection and loss to move through this framework to reach the redemption phase. This is not a tidy, linear process but rather phases that we can expect to travel through, if we want to take the mess and turn it into a message.

Let's explore *authenticity.* Most dictionaries agree that *authenticity* is defined as the quality of being an established authority of being truthful and correct; the quality of being original and not corrupted.

There are many articles online about the value of authenticity within business, but I have chosen to draw from Heather MacArthur's article in Forbes magazine about what authenticity is and how to use it. Despite once having lost work due to authenticity, she advocates being authentic to build trust with your clients. I am going to highlight a couple of points she makes, due to space, but I recommend a further read.

Heather MacArthur speaks of the importance of taking time to know ourselves. Self and other awareness is an asset for our businesses and well worth the investment. She also stresses the importance of developing one's own viewpoint. Investment in coaching can allow us time to clearly prepare and articulate our authentic view as opposed to simply going with the current trend. She also believes that conformity does not equate to success. Business ideas need innovative ideas that require authenticity. Finally, she mentions that we need to know what stories drive our behaviour (MacArthur). Again, coaching or counselling can help this.

As Christ's followers, the Bible is central to our thinking and actions. Here are four passages that speak to an aspect of authenticity:

Passage 1: Authenticity Involves Showing Christ's Love

"Through the Lord's mercies we are not consumed, because His compassions fail not. They are new every morning; great is Your faithfulness. 'The Lord is my portion,' says my soul, 'therefore I hope in Him.'" -Lamentations 3:22–23, NKJV

In the original Hebrew, "hesed" (Hebrew meaning loyal love) includes loving-kindness, mercy, and covenant love, which is deeper and stronger than anything outside of Christ (Schroeder). Authentic Christ followers are to display the 'hesed' love in all areas of life.

Passage 2: Authenticity Means Abiding In Christ

"Abide in Me, and I in you. As the branch cannot bear fruit of itself, unless it abides in the vine, neither can you, unless you abide in Me. I am the vine, you are the branches. He who abides in Me, and I in him, bears much fruit; for without Me you can do nothing." -John 15:4-6, NKJV

Passage 3: Authenticity Means Renewing Our Minds

"And do not be conformed to this world, but be transformed by the renewing of your mind, that you may prove what is that good and acceptable and perfect will of God."
-Romans 12:2, NKJV

Passage 4: Authenticity means honouring our bodies

"Do you not know that your bodies are temples of the Holy Spirit, who is in you, whom you have received from God? You are not your own; you were bought at a price. Therefore honour God with your bodies." - 1 Corinthians 6:19-20, NIV

From a Biblical perspective, loving, abiding, renewing our mind, and honouring God with our bodies are all aspects of authenticity. The first letter in each of these points spell LAMB (Love, Abide, Mind, Body). Lambs are cared for by shepherds. As we allow God to be our Shepherd in our lives and businesses then He leads, and we follow, and the order is the right way round.

I believe we have a promise from Psalm 1:3 that provided we let God lead and we follow that whatever we do will prosper.

"And he shall be like a tree planted by the rivers of water, that bringeth forth his fruit in his season; his leaf also shall not wither; and whatsoever he doeth shall prosper"-Psalm 1:3, KJV.

Within my business, I am learning to grow in my own communication with God so that He is leading. I seek to listen to God and then do what he says. If I get the order wrong, then I adjust what I am doing. Mark Virkler is a pastor who spent a year seeking to discover how to recognise the voice. His book *4 Keys to Hearing God's Voice* covers the following four keys: quieting yourself down, focusing on Jesus, tuning into spontaneity, and journaling (Virkler). This is a practice that I have used and am seeking to use again because otherwise, I find myself having to adjust because I have rushed ahead of God's plans.

Business principles do not work in isolation. We are all in business to grow and develop our businesses. Gino Chirio, in *The Harvard Business Review* suggests six ways to grow a business. Gino refers to innovating with new processes, experiences, features, customers, offerings, and models, which includes connecting with customers (Chirio). In a world full of masks, increasing authentic connection creates trust. One of my clients has given me permission to share the value of authenticity within coaching with Radiant Destiny so that she could move forward in her life and business:

"When I met Chris I was emotionally stuck and drowning in my head with overwhelm. I wanted to break free from the prison of my mind and fulfil my goals and destiny that God had for my life but after many negative situations and relationships I needed someone that could help me look at things from a different perspective. Chris allowed me to be real, to her and to myself. It was only with that authenticity that I could move forward."

Tanya Harris, Business Owner, Australia (2023)

AUTHENTICITY IN BUSINESS-EXPRESSED IN THREE WAYS

AUTHENTICITY IN PERSONAL GROWTH:

Those who want to grow in their sense of value, identity and God-given purpose as individuals or empower others to do so. God's VIP's was formed for professional helpers and individuals to grow knowing their value, identity and purpose and fulfilling it so that the bigger, better, bolder God-given dreams become a reality. When we are aware of our value, identity, and purpose it makes it easier for us to authentically relate to our client's needs.

AUTHENTICITY IN FUTURE PLANNING:

There are three areas beginning with the letter A that will help you see authenticity in your future planning: authenticity, alignment, and assignment. This will take your life or business to the next level as you plan for the future.

Authenticity - Destruction to Radical Destiny

Authenticity in Communication Development:

This is also known as *rapportful communication* where we learn how to communicate more easily. We communicate with ourselves, with others and if we are believers, we communicate with God. Each area can be enhanced because so much misunderstanding and distance is created by communication problems.

Here are some top tips for growing authenticity from where you are now:

Align Personal Values And Business Practices

Sometimes the values espoused by a company are not seen in practice and this impedes authentic communication. For me, at the prospect stage, I check whether the clients' values and mine align so that I can work with them. If values are not aligned, I refer them to someone else. My values include honesty, encouragement, authenticity, and love which spell out the word *HEAL*. Being authentic in itself is a healing way to show up in business. There are lists of values online that could be used to scan through and consider which ones sit well with you such as the Harris list (Selig).

BUILD SELF-AWARENESS AND COMMUNICATION SKILLS

I have invested heavily in my own personal development throughout my life so that I know myself better and can then authentically share with others. I also invested in learning how to extend my communication skills with a wider range of people through the multiple coaching programmes and certifications I have acquired in Neurolinguistic Programming, with a Christian provider and the International Coach Academy.

Investment in our personal development, growth and communication skills can not only enable us to grow as individuals but it also allows us to express our true selves and build rapport with a wider range of people more freely. This investment can be in the form of group or individual coaching, counselling, or investing in diagnostic tools with feedback from those who know us. Personally, it was the latter that confirmed that I had the skills to write courses to help others grow. Anonymous feedback from those who knew me was an integral part which was useful.

Creating solutions to business problems based on your own uniqueness requires recognition of a person's unique offering and an acceptance of diversity. A unique selling point can be developed from our own story or unique set of interests, values, skills, and passions. This can be seen in the marketing strategies used. Increasingly, business owners are encouraged to use relatable "real photos" because customers want to trust that the service is real and not fake. By using photos that are as real as possible and not photoshopped, this is believed by many, in itself, to build relatability and trust.

I strongly recommend you setting aside time to reflect on the following questions so that you can implement greater authenticity into your life and business.

Questions For Reflection

What is the first step you could take in your personal development journey, on the basis that the more you invest in YOU, the more you invest in your business? Are you willing to invest in yourself and/or your team?

From the Biblical passages above, covering love, abiding, renewing the mind and honouring your body, which one do you feel needs attention first and is likely to make the most difference? What is the first small step to take?

I encourage you to reflect and journal for 5 minutes on each of the following:

    a) Your value
    b) Your identity
    c) Your purpose

How easy or otherwise difficult is this to do?

Write down 5 sentences in response to a, b, and c that you can revisit later. Knowing your value, identity, and purpose as God's VIP, allows you to authentically communicate clearly with others because you are sure of yourself.

Authenticity, alignment, and assignment are closely linked.

- What are your top four values in life and business?
- How are they reflected in your business practices and your life in general?
- How could you communicate more authentically and effectively with prospects and clients?
- How can we display *hesed* (love) to our clients and colleagues?
- What simple additional actions could you take or what could you adjust in your personal life or business so that others see the authentic you and quickly build trust with you?

If you are committed to being an authentic professional who effectively empowers others in your team, business, or ministry, then growing in authenticity is essential. Do you want to build a business in which authenticity runs through your values, actions, marketing, and business practices so that values and practices are clear, authentic, and aligned? Do you want to inspire women to know their value, identity, and God-given purpose? Do you want to develop authentic positive communication both internally, with others, and with God which builds trust with clients? Can you afford to drift and lose time, NOT overcome overwhelm, NOT break free from imposter syndrome, and achieve less than your God-given calling or mandate? Can you afford NOT to grow into Christ displaying His love, abiding in Him, renewing your mind, and honouring him with your body?

Now is the time. None of us know if we have tomorrow and our time is finite.

Dean Graziosi, personal development trainer with Tony Robbins, encourages people to take *uncomfortable action* in line with their goal. This has worked for him and for me! It may be uncomfortable to be authentic. We need to take time to identify our purpose and make the changes that allow us to grow into fulfilling our God-given purpose.

ABOUT THE AUTHOR

Chris Porter is a strategist, visionary, pioneering coach, teacher, counsellor, motivating facilitator as well as a Mum and a friend. She has lived in the UK and the USA and has friends from Malawi serving their community with the Tengani Foundation tirelessly to bring relief and hope. Her family experience includes marriage, singleness, motherhood and facing dementia through the experiences of both her late parents. She is now considering the legacy she wants to leave for future generations, which has caused her to contribute to this book.

She has a passion for people to know their intrinsic, inherent, God-given worth, personal identity through God's eyes and to fulfil their true purpose in life with joy, overcoming grief and obstacles with grace, faith, hope and determination.

Chris often hears people say she inspires them. It is her freely given faith at her core which makes her resilient and courageous as well as the lives her late parents modelled with missionary zeal. Knowing her value, identity, and purpose has enabled her to fight through imposter syndrome and self-doubt to learn the skills to set up a business to serve her clients

Whether you have a business idea, an existing business, or want to incorporate authenticity more intentionally into your business to take it to the next level I would like to leave you with a personal challenge and encouragement: Only you can do what you were created to do! Together each achieve more! Invest 30 minutes with me and see where that takes you!

"Therefore, my beloved brethren, be steadfast, immovable, always abounding in the work of the Lord, knowing that your labour is not in vain in the Lord" - 1 Corinthians 15:58, NKJV.

TO CONNECT WITH CHRIS:

Email: chris@cjporter.com
LinkedIn linkedin.com/in/radiantdestinyservices

CHAPTER 12

Faith is Key

Mary Westcott, USA
POSTPARTUM DEPRESSION COACH

Life as a mom, podcast host, and business owner is challenging. I have faced challenges such as overwhelm due to stress and self-doubt as I was building my podcast and business. I stayed consistent with content building and scheduling my episodes until I started to get burnt out by adding too many tasks to my agenda. As a business owner and mother working a nine-to-five job. I was busy six days per week. I did not set the boundaries between motherhood, adulthood, and business when I should have. While I was juggling the business side of content building or keeping an organized schedule for an easy flow, I was also trying to take care of my children, run errands, do chores, and make sure the home had order in place. Little did I know, I was crumbling at my own feet. I was waking up angry at the world, hating myself, and feeling like a failure for three full years. People told me to never bring work home. Do you know what? They were right! That was another challenge I faced, which resulted in wanting to give up. I started to notice a shift in my mindset and feelings, and my perspective on life had changed for the worse. I knew I had to change because it is not who I am, it is not who God created me to be, and I missed feeling joyful, happy, and loved. As I prayed to God, I asked Him if He could give me the strength and knowledge to get out of this terrible funk. He answered me with the vision of having my own podcast navigating through the postpartum depression journey I was on after reading about a first-time mother, who was approximately the same age as me, who committed suicide due to postpartum depression. That was when I knew who to serve and how to do it. That was when *The Fearless Mom Tribe* podcast was born. Since I started that journey, I have received so much love from different mothers who have similar struggles. I also learned about different challenges other mothers face such as having children with ADHD, suicide from drugs, and mothers in domestic violence cases, and how they were able to get out just in time. God showed me how a powerful pain story can rescue others. I am also becoming a life coach for mothers who suffer from postpartum depression because I believe there is not enough conversation or helpful resources on what to expect, what to look out for, and how to start your own healing process with practical strategies.

There are so many reasons why I have started my podcast and why I have taken the steps to become an author. The urge to start my business was from all the major pains I have gone through as a young working adult and a new expecting mother. I was born and raised in Des Moines, Iowa until I graduated high school. In the same year, I moved out with just me and my clothes to a small town in Iowa that was two and a half hours away; no family, no friends, just a teenager who was ready to start living and experiencing new opportunities. I was aware of racial tension. My parents taught us early on what that looks like through conversations you have with people, and the mannerisms people portray. I dealt with racial discrimination and profiling as soon as I had my first job at the age of sixteen. It wasn't anything new to me until I started at a factory five and a half years ago. I have gone through numerous situations that dealt with racial discrimination, harassment, and unfair advantages to the point that I had to fight to keep my job. For example, I had people try to fire me by writing up statements about how I said things or even how I presented myself towards them. I faced racism because of the color of my skin, who I was married to, and how I was growing my family. I faced quite a bit of racial comments where I questioned if I was doing the right thing to start a family. I doubted my work ethic and who I was as a person. I prayed and prayed and prayed to God to give me a sign and the strength to get me through the hardships I was facing.

I woke up one morning and had this sense of motivation and determination. I knew the obstacles I went through and was facing were going to be the power to my success. As I mentioned before, I had postpartum depression. I was going through all the emotions and thoughts you could imagine while going up against people who did not care for me and what I was about. I faked it until I made it. As I prayed, God led me to fight for the power I had lost. What fueled me was understanding I had a purpose, and as long as I had faith and believed God would pull me through to the other side, all things would come to pass as they should. As I was working my nine-to-five, I would get blank pieces of paper and work on podcast ideas, such as content to post and my next episodes. That helped me to remain in good spirits: positive and hopeful. On weekends I would sit down in my office, and outline what my next steps were going to be to become a successful podcast host. I would write out my vision, my mission, and my "why." I would record myself and speak things into existence, so when I looked back, I could see how far I have come. I tackled my mindset. As many of you know, it all starts within, and your mind is powerful. I did not want my thoughts and the circumstances I was facing to control me. I woke up every morning remembering why I was doing this and who I was doing it for. I am doing this for the moms who face PPD (postpartum depression), who are seeking support, love, and answers to the madness of motherhood, and I am doing this for my children. I am creating a legacy my children can look back on and say their mother moved mountains for them to have a greater life with the grace and love of God. As I step into the purpose that God has laid out for me, I have found that podcasting and writing my first book allowed me to see my vision and serve my moms in a better way. I want to help moms who cannot help themselves or who are looking for a little boost to help them keep going. Not only am I growing my podcast and becoming an author, but God has helped me become a state-certified childcare provider, which has led me to leave my nine-to-five job for good.

Faith is Key

I made a promise to myself that I would not go back to that place no matter what happens and God has made a way. Starting my own childcare business, I realized that it is the next stepping stone that will allow me to become a full-time entrepreneur. I can create my own hours and join business meetings. I wasn't able to do that in the past and can be with my babies full time.

I love what I do. My podcast and daycare are avenues to show moms that there are people out there who truly care for them and their children. I want to go beyond the stereotype that daycare providers are only in it for the money. I want to show them I would take care of and love their children just like I would love my own. I want to share my story with the world and let people know they are not alone when they face certain circumstances in their lives. I can relate and understand and am here to help where I can.

As adults, we are programmed to do things for others before ourselves, but in reality, we have to help ourselves and fill our cups before others sometimes. If we don't, we will burn out with overwhelm and exhaustion. God wants us to be warriors and people to spread love and helpfulness through our purpose. My daycare and podcast helped me overcome the challenges I have faced through racial discrimination by helping me find my voice to speak about the situations I went through and how I was able to conquer them by walking with God on my healing journey. It also helped me to dive into figuring out who I am as a person, a mother, a wife, and an entrepreneur. It gave me back my confidence when realizing what my core values are and how important they are to me. I also realized that my coworkers were envious when it came to performing my duties at work. They would give me a dirty look because I worked side by side with my husband. I had one co-worker come up to me and say, "You know, many people were hoping that you didn't get the job in this department, right?" I also had HR have a private meeting with my husband and me and said, "We do not want any problems being caused, because you two are married. If we suspect anything, your supervisors will separate you two." As every last little comment rolled in like a tidal wave, it started to affect me. I allowed myself to get influenced by the negative comments, which blinded me from seeing the true traits of myself that God has blessed me with, such as having confidence in myself, commitment, loyalty, and being dependable as not only an employee but as a co-worker. When I figured that out, I knew what needed to be done. It was time to take back my power as a creative,

FAITH IS KEY

unique, bold, and God-fearing woman. That is what I am here to do and that is what keeps me going.

My podcast stands out from all other podcasts and books because I hone in on helping moms who face postpartum depression overcome those dark times and step into the light of their full purpose. I help them to recognize they are not *just* moms in this world, but they are individuals who have a purpose, a passion, and a dream that needs to be shared with the world. When you follow Kingdom principles and implement them into your business, it separates you from all other businesses by your uniqueness. I put faith in my business. When there is faith, you are building trust with God to lead you through the hard times. As a podcast host, when I put faith into my episodes, I trust God will provide true and genuine listeners who can relate to the topics I talk about. When I interview different guests, I allow God to do His work to bless me with guests who will help my listeners gain the knowledge and support that they need through the stories each guest shares. My podcast stands out from other podcasts because I have a unique style of how I present myself, the topics I share, and the guests I bring. My book stands out from all other books because the topic I share is not one that society talks about or wants to face. God has given me the vision, confidence, and knowledge to find a way to get my story out into the world in different forms to help those who can relate. When you put certain principles into your business, such as faith, perseverance, integrity, or dedication, it will bring out your strengths, weaknesses, and lessons you will learn along the way. For example, with faith, my strong points are prayer and trust in God. When I pray, I know that God is listening, and He will show up on time all the time. That is where trusting in Him comes in. You have to know that He will be there for you instead of you wanting results right away. Just know that He is always there, and He hears you. When you consider that, you will be able to strive and conquer the challenging parts of your business a lot better.

We all have weaknesses and my weakness with faith is to continue praying and trusting in God when I face different challenges along the way. We all have those moments where we feel discouraged, helpless, or lonely because of different situations in our lives: a death in the family, finances, or something internal like feeling overwhelmed and burned out. I have had a great challenge to keep pursuing and staying dedicated when obstacles come my way. Take a step back and analyze what is happening and what you need right in that very moment. It might be sleep, getting in touch with God through prayer, reading the Bible, or simply taking a break. You will be able to come back with a new mind and a new heart to face the challenge head-on. God will provide, bless, and show you what you are simply missing, what needs to be worked on, and how you can expand a little better. God gave me the challenge that I never knew I needed to continue to build my brand. I learned different ways to present myself by expanding from podcasting to writing a book. Having faith in my business helped me grow my audience and meet the people who mentor me. It also allowed me to become a mentor for others. Following Kingdom principles will open doors of opportunity for you and your business, but first, you want to sit down and think about your strengths and weaknesses, and the knowledge you want to gain in your business. When you start with that process, you will have a clear understanding of how to build your foundation, know your next step, and get clear on your purpose, who you serve, and how to do it. Adding God to all your plans and strategies is the icing on the cake. When you allow God to show you where to go, you will be surprised at the opportunities waiting for you!

The Kingdom principle I want to apply more in my business is living by faith. When you have faith in things you do or want to do, it motivates you to achieve those goals even if life throws you a curve ball. It gives you the perseverance you never had. When you have faith in God and put Him into your business through prayer by talking with Him, He will bless you with the knowledge you never knew you were missing. He will give you the ideas to help you to get out of that slump you have been in for weeks and He knows what you need when starting a brand new venture. He will supply you with those ingredients one by one to create that masterpiece that is ready for the world to see. Faith goes a long way when you want to start a business for the first time. It gives you the bravery to take the first step when there is no one in your corner to cheer you on. For those who have been in business for a while, faith will help you keep going when fear tries to peek around the corner and throw you off track. It brings back the reassurance that you can do all things through Christ who strengthens you. The Lord will not steer you in the wrong lane. He will provide the right path for you when facing hardships. Faith can be the foundation when building your business because as a child of God, you must include Him in all you do. Having faith has allowed me to get out of my comfort zone and take the challenge to see my full potential as a whole.

Faith is Key

I was extremely scared to start my podcast and to become an author. I did not know where to start, what to do, or what type of resources I needed, but God walked with me the entire way and showed me what I needed to do. Building my business through faith has allowed me to persevere in the hardest of times when negative thoughts and feelings rise to the surface of my soul. I did not let it consume me, but I walked through it and tried to understand what God was wanting me to learn in that moment. When you have faith and use it as your foundation in building your business, it will open doors to opportunities you would never even think would be possible. For example, with this opportunity, being able to collaborate with amazing authors in this book, I never would have thought I would be an author. I am working on my own book as well, which is exciting and such a blessing to experience. I have always loved writing, but I never thought it was for me, due to people around me, who doubted the ideas I had as a young child. The same is true for podcasting. I love to talk but never would have thought I would create one or know if I would have any listeners. I took the risk even with fear and self-doubt, and I proved myself (and others) wrong. God has shown me when you work hard, listen, and have faith in Him, He will provide so much more than you expect. Having faith is such an important principle because in the hard times, it will help you keep pushing through and lean on God more. The benefits of building faith in your business are having a stronger bond with God, moving into your full purpose, building more confidence within yourself, stepping out of your comfort zone, and challenging yourself. When you have faith, it will allow you to expand your knowledge by networking with individuals who are a few steps ahead of you but are willing to give you the proper advice and knowledge you need. As a podcast host, I have learned so much from others who have been on my show. I even learned from other podcasters how to simplify certain backend procedures when going into the editing process. God has given me people to better myself, learn more, and to be able to teach others the things I have learned. I was blessed with having a mindset coach who brought out the confidence in me. I was also able to have a business coach for the first time. I was taught different marketing strategies, how to get myself more visible, and how to expand on the brand I was creating. I was able to invest in a book coach to help me get my story out into the world on paper.

Faith is so important when having your business and I cannot say it enough. The works of God will show through you by how you present yourself and your business to others. Faith helps with the decision-making process and the marketing side as well when it comes to clients or as a podcaster in finding the right interviewee. When it comes to faith in God, you need to believe He will carry you through your business in the best way. You only need the size of a mustard seed. You know the saying, *"You can accomplish anything if you put your mind to it?"* That quote describes faith. Knowing faith will pull you through will help you get over the obstacles that you are facing. Having faith is that powerful. He will provide and bless you more than you will know. When I share my story with the world through podcasting, I help other moms find my podcast by sharing it with them through social media groups or making enticing posts. I create a call to action at the end of every episode that tells them to leave a rating and share it with their friends and family members. I network and connect with other moms in business who are looking for the next best podcast of their interest. As a business owner, you have to put yourself out into the world, whether it scares you or not. So, I got out of my comfort zone and went on other podcasts that had a mom audience. I shared my postpartum depression story and talked about how it helped me turn my hardships into accomplishments.

A few strategies that can help you implement faith into your business are prayer, journaling, and practicing gratitude.

PRAYER

Prayer has helped me build a strong bond with God. I call it, "the silent journal." This is where you can just talk with Him, ask questions, and ask Him to help you gain the strength, courage, and motivation to strive better with your business. Prayer goes a long way, and it works. God has given me the strength to keep pushing through my day, week, and months. I know He can help you too.

JOURNALING

Journaling is a great way to keep focused on your personal and business goals. Sometimes we will feel overwhelmed with so much and that is where journaling comes into play.

YOU CAN JOURNAL ABOUT:

- All that comes to your mind.
- What you are feeling at that moment?
- The likes and dislikes of your day.

Here is a tip when journaling to gain a positive outcome: write out all the negative thoughts and emotions you can. Then you want to write a positive passage to fill you up. I found out that when you talk about amazing dreams, goals, or even your vision, it will give you the excitement and the reminder of *why* you started in the first place.

GRATITUDE

Another strategy that helps you to build faith in your business is practicing gratitude.

- Create a gratitude list.
- What are you grateful and/or thankful for?
- What makes you happy?
- What are the little things that keep you grounded and whole?
- What are the top five most important things or people in your life and why?

When you practice gratitude, you will find the little things that are placed right in front of you that God has given you as a blessing. It will signal a reminder of your *why* (why you started), your *where* (where you are going), your *how* (how did you get here), and the *who* (who has helped you, supported you and is still in your corner). When you acknowledge those simple points, the negative thoughts that creep in will disappear and not matter anymore. For example: I am so grateful for God because He has woken me up to start a new day, a new way to share, network, and shine in other people's lives. He has given me my little family who have supported me through my entrepreneurial journey.

My children are my reason I want the best life for them to live. God has shown me where I am when remember the past pain, trials, and tribulations I have gone through because of postpartum depression, racial discrimination, and doubt. The pain I suffered in my past has helped me to get to where I am today; to create helpful resources, support, and love for the moms whom I serve. Faith will allow you to truly find your purpose, and the resources for others who are facing certain hardships for which you might have the answers. This only happens when you have full faith in God.

In your business, always remember that it is okay to take a break. Give yourself grace, love, and respect. Sometimes, God wants you to rest rather than work. When having faith, God will speak to you and tell you what is best for you. Sometimes resting is what you will need to succeed. Rest in faith.

ABOUT THE AUTHOR

Mary Westcott is a stay-at-home mother who owns her state-registered in-home childcare business. She is also a respite worker who works with children who have mental challenges. She is a mother and has two beautiful daughters. Mary is a wife to a supportive husband who has been by her side through all her business ventures. She is an entrepreneur who wears many hats such as being a podcast host, an author, and a life coach for moms who suffer from postpartum depression. Mary loves to read, write, listen to music, and crochet. If she is not working on her business or enjoying her hobbies, you can find her spending time with her family and friends by going out to eat, walking trails, enjoying nature, or going on family trips. Mary is in the transition to building a stronger relationship with God every day through prayer, listening to gospel music, and reading scriptures.

To Connect with Mary:

Email: *maryw@momswhoslay.co*
Instagram: @moms.whoslay
Website: *www.momswhoslay.co*

Other Books:

Rise Above: Empowering moms to slay postpartum depression and reclaim their strength

Works Cited

Adao, Pedro. *www.pedroadao.com*. n.d. Field of Favor Workbook, Day 5, 2020 - 100X Academy Training.

Bynes, Shae. *https://kingdomdrivenentrepreneur.com*. n.d. Audio Recording - Firestarter School - Day 1.

Capps, Charles. *https://cappsministries.com/products/the-dominion-principle#:~:*. n.d. CD.

Chirio, Gino. "https://hbr.org/2018/06/the-6-ways-to-grow-a-company." 2018. *Harvard Business Review*.

MacArthur, Heather V. "https://www.forbes.com/sites/hvmacarthur/2020/02/21/authenticity-what-is-it-how-do-you-have-it-how-should-you-use-it." 2020. *Forbes.com*.

Schroeder, Sylvia. "https://www.christianity.com/wiki/christian-terms/what-is-hesed-love-and-what-does-it-tell-us-about-gods-love-for-us.html." n.d.

Selig, Meg. "https://www.psychologytoday.com/ca/blog/changepower/201811/6-ways-discover-and-choose-your-core-values." 2018. *https://www.psychologytoday.com*. Blog .

Virkler, Mark. *4 Keys to Hearing God's Voice*. Destiny Image, Incorporated, 2010.

New Collaborative Book

Coming Soon

JANUARY 2025

If you would like an opportunity to be a part of a collaborative book where you'll get to share the Kingdom wisdom imparted to you in your life, then *Tell Your Story: How He turned my pain into purpose* is for you! Email below for more information.

If you would like to write, self-publish, launch a business, or market your solo Kingdom book, please email
connect@network4thekingdom.com
Subject line: COLLAB BOOK or SOLO BOOK

Join our free Books to Business community for tips, updates, connections, and more

Network for the Kingdom
Purpose-Promise-Profit

N4K

Follow Us On
YouTube

Join Our
Free Community
on Facebook